STRIDE TOWARD FREEDOM

The Montgomery Story

Stride Toward FREEDOM

The Montgomery Story

BY MARTIN LUTHER KING, JR

1817

HARPER & ROW, PUBLISHERS, SAN FRANCISCO

*Cambridge, Hagerstown, New York, Philadelphia, Washington
London, Mexico City, São Paulo, Singapore, Sydney*

A hardcover edition of this book was published by Harper & Row, Publishers, Inc.

Photographs on page 65, top and lower right of page 167: copyright © 1958 by Wide World Photos.

Photographs on pages 66-68, 165-166, and bottom of 168: copyright © 1958 by Dan Weiner.

Library of Congress Cataloging in Publication Data
King, Martin Luther Jr.

    Stride toward freedom: the montgomery story
    I. Title

                                                  58-7099

ISBN 0-06-250490-8

---

86 87 88 89 90 **MPC** 10 9 8 7 6 5 4 3 2 1

To Coretta
my beloved wife and co-worker

Contents

Preface

T<small>HIS</small> book is an account of a few years that changed the life of a Southern community, told from the point of view of one of the participants. Although it attempts to interpret what happened it does not purport to be a detailed survey of the historical and sociological aspects of the Montgomery story. It is therefore limited in scope and its point of view is inevitably personal.

While the nature of this account causes me to make frequent use of the pronoun "I," in every important part of the story it should be "we." This is not a drama with only one actor. More precisely it is the chronicle of 50,000 Negroes who took to heart the principles of nonviolence, who learned to fight for their rights with the weapon of love, and who, in the process, acquired a new estimate of their own human worth. It is the story of Negro leaders of many faiths and divided allegiances, who came together in the bond of a cause they knew was right. And of the Negro followers, many of them beyond middle age, who walked to work and home again as much as twelve miles a day for over a year rather than submit to the discourtesies and humiliation of segregated buses. The majority of the Negroes who took part in the year-long boycott of Montgomery's buses were poor and untutored; but they understood the essence of the Montgomery movement. One elderly woman summed it up for the rest. When asked after several weeks of walking whether she was tired, she answered, "My feets is tired, but my soul is at rest."

There is another side to the picture: it is the white community of Montgomery, long led or intimidated by a few extremists, that finally turned in disgust on the perpetrators of crime in the name of segregation. The change should not be exaggerated. The White Citizens Council is still active. Confessed bombers still win their freedom in the courts. And opposition to integration is still the rule. Yet by the end of the bus struggle it was clear that the vast majority of Montgomery's whites preferred peace and law to the excesses performed in the name of segregation. And even though the many saw segregation as right because it was the tradition, there were always the courageous few who saw the injustice in segregation and fought against it side by side with the Negroes.

Since Montgomery, a gallant bus protest has been conducted in Tallahassee, and efforts to integrate buses have spread to many other Southern communities. Negroes throughout the South have begun to take up in earnest their right to register and vote. Little Rock has occurred, and Negro children have walked with fortitude through the ranks of white students—often hostile and jeering—at Central High School. How much the Montgomery movement helped to give strength and new courage to Negroes elsewhere, and how much Montgomery and Little Rock and Tallahassee were all results of the same causes, is a matter for future historians. Whatever the final estimate, it is already clear that Montgomery was a part of something much larger than itself.

The problem of acknowledgments in a work of this sort is immense. How can one acknowledge 50,000 individual contributions? Yet the book would not be complete without the author's thanks to some of the many people who made it possible.

I am deeply grateful to Theodore Brown, Charles Gomillion, Lewis Wade Jones, and Harris Wofford for significant suggestions and real encouragement. They are not responsible for my failure to accomplish all for which they must have hoped.

I am also indebted to my teacher and friend George D. Kelsey, who has given me valuable and stimulating suggestions.

I am sincerely grateful to my close associates, Mrs. Jo Ann Robinson and Fred D. Gray, for a painstaking and detailed reading of the entire manuscript.

My thanks also go to my friend L. D. Reddick who has read the manuscript and provided both suggestions and materials of rare usefulness. I am especially grateful to Mrs. Hermine Popper of Harper & Brothers, who with great competence rendered invaluable editorial assistance.

I am indebted to my secretary, Mrs. Maude Ballou, who continually encouraged me to persevere in this work and with great toil transferred my handwritten pages to typewritten copy.

I thank, too, my collegemate Elliot Finley and his wife Genevieve, who provided a quiet and comfortable home where most of these words were written.

I owe a special debt of gratitude to the press—especially to Ted Poston of the *New York Post*, Abel Plenn of *The New York Times*, and Norman Walton of *The Negro History Bulletin*—whose reports of Montgomery provided invaluable resources and stimulants to my memory.

I am deeply grateful to the members of the Dexter Avenue Baptist Church, without whose patience, loyalty, and encouragement the completion of this work would not have been possible.

Most of all I am indebted to my wife Coretta, without whose love, sacrifices, and loyalty neither life nor work would bring fulfillment. She has given me words of consolation when I needed

them most and a well-ordered home where Christian love is a
reality. To her the book is dedicated.

MARTIN LUTHER KING, JR.

Montgomery, Alabama
May, 1958

STRIDE TOWARD FREEDOM

The Montgomery Story

I

Return to the South

On a cool Saturday afternoon in January 1954, I set out to drive from Atlanta, Georgia, to Montgomery, Alabama. It was a clear wintry day. The Metropolitan Opera was on the radio with a performance of one of my favorite operas—Donizetti's *Lucia di Lammermoor*. So with the beauty of the countryside, the inspiration of Donizetti's inimitable music, and the splendor of the skies, the usual monotony that accompanies a relatively long drive—especially when one is alone—was dispelled in pleasant diversions.

After a few hours I drove through rich and fertile farmlands to the sharp bend in the Alabama River on whose shores Montgomery stands. Although I had passed through the city before, I had never been there on a real visit. Now I would have the opportunity to spend a few days in this beautiful little city, one of the oldest in the United States.

Not long after I arrived a friend took me to see the Dexter Avenue Baptist Church where I was to preach the following morning. A solid brick structure erected in Reconstruction days, it stood at one corner of a handsome square not far from the center of town. As we drove up to the church I noticed diagonally across the square a stately white building of impressive proportions and arresting beauty, the State Capitol. The present building was erected in 1851, and its high-domed central portion is one of the finest examples of classical Georgian architecture in America. Here on January 7, 1861, Alabama voted to secede from the Union, and on February 18, on the steps of the portico, Jefferson Davis took his oath of office as President of the Confederate States. It is for this reason that Montgomery has been known across the years as the Cradle of the Confederacy. Here the first Confederate flag was made and unfurled. One could see many of the patterns of the old Confederacy and the ante-bellum tradition persisting in Montgomery today, alongside the lively evidence of modern economic development.

I was to see this imposing reminder of the Confederacy from the steps of the Dexter Avenue Baptist Church many times in the following years; for my visit in January proved to be a prelude to my coming to live in Montgomery.

The previous August of 1953, after being in school twenty-one years without a break, I had reached the satisfying moment of completing the residential requirements for the Ph.D. degree. The major job that remained was to write my doctoral thesis. In the meantime I had felt that it would be wise to start considering a job so that I could be placed at least by September 1954. Two churches in the East—one in Massachusetts and one in New York —had expressed an interest in calling me. Three colleges had offered me attractive and challenging posts—one a teaching post, one a deanship, and the other an administrative position. In the midst of thinking about each of these positions, I had received a letter from the officers of the Dexter Avenue Baptist Church of Montgomery, saying that they were without a pastor and that they would be glad to have me preach when I was again in that section of the country. The officers who extended the invitation had heard of me through my father in Atlanta and other ministerial friends. I had written immediately saying that I would be home in Atlanta for the Christmas holidays, and that I would be happy to come to Montgomery to preach one Sunday in January.

The church was comparatively small, with a membership of around three hundred people, but it occupied a central place in the community. Many influential and respected citizens—professional people with substantial incomes—were among its members. Moreover it had a long tradition of an educated ministry. Some of the nation's best-trained Negro ministers had held pastorates there.

That Saturday evening as I began going over my sermon, I was aware of a certain anxiety. Although I had preached many times before—having served as associate pastor of my father's church in Atlanta for four years, and having done all of the preaching there for three successive summers—I was very conscious this time that I was on trial. How could I best impress the congregation? Since the membership was educated and intelligent, should I attempt to interest it with a display of scholarship? Or should I preach just as I had always done, depending finally on the inspiration of the spirit of God? I decided to follow the latter course. I said to myself, "Keep Martin Luther King in the background and God in the foreground and everything will be all right. Remember you are a channel of the gospel and not the source."

At eleven o'clock on Sunday I was in the pulpit, delivering my sermon before a large congregation. My topic was: "The Three Dimensions of a Complete Life." The congregation was receptive, and I left with the feeling that God had used me well, and that here was a fine church with challenging possibilities. Later in the day the pulpit committee talked to me concerning many business details of the church, and asked me if I would accept the pastorate in the event they saw fit to call me. After answering that I would give such a call my most prayerful and serious consideration, I left Montgomery for Atlanta, and then took a flight back to Boston.

About a month later I received an air-mail, special-delivery letter from Montgomery, telling me that I had been unanimously called to the pastorate of the Dexter Avenue Baptist Church. I was very happy to have this offer, but I did not answer immediately; for I was to fly to Detroit the next morning for a preaching engagement the following Sunday.

It was one of those turbulent days in which the clouds hovered low, but as the plane lifted itself above the weather, the choppiness of the flight soon passed. As I watched the silvery sheets of clouds below and the deep dark shadow of the blue above, I faced up to the problem of what to do about the several offers that had come my way. At this time I was torn in two directions. On the one hand I was inclined toward the pastorate; on the other hand, toward educational work. Which way should I go? And if I accepted a church, should it be one in the South, with all the tragic implications of segregation, or one of the two available pulpits in the North?

As far back as I could remember, I had resented segregation, and had asked my parents urgent and pointed questions about it. While I was still too young for school I had already learned something about discrimination. For three or four years my inseparable playmates had been two white boys whose parents ran a store across the street from our home in Atlanta. Then something began to happen. When I went across the street to get them, their parents would say that they couldn't play. They weren't hostile; they just made excuses. Finally I asked my mother about it.

Every parent at some time faces the problem of explaining the facts of life to his child. Just as inevitably, for the Negro parent, the moment comes when he must explain to his offspring the facts of segregation. My mother took me on her lap and began by telling me about slavery and how it had ended with the Civil War. She tried to explain the divided system of the South—the segregated schools, restaurants, theaters, housing; the white and colored signs on drinking fountains, waiting rooms, lavatories— as a social condition rather than a natural order. Then she said the words that almost every Negro hears before he can yet understand the injustice that makes them necessary: "You are as good as anyone."

My mother, as the daughter of a successful minister, had grown up in comparative comfort. She had been sent to the best available school and college and had, in general, been protected from the worst blights of discrimination. But my father, a sharecropper's son, had met its brutalities at first hand, and had begun to strike back at an early age. With his fearless honesty and his robust, dynamic presence, his words commanded attention.

I remembered a trip to a downtown shoestore with Father when I was still small. We had sat down in the first empty seats at the front of the store. A young white clerk came up and murmured politely:

"I'll be happy to wait on you if you'll just move to those seats in the rear."

My father answered, "There's nothing wrong with these seats. We're quite comfortable here."

"Sorry," said the clerk, "but you'll have to move."

"We'll either buy shoes sitting here," my father retorted, "or we won't buy shoes at all." Whereupon he took me by the hand and walked out of the store. This was the first time I had ever seen my father so angry. I still remember walking down the street beside him as he muttered, "I don't care how long I have to live with this system, I will never accept it,"

And he never has. I remembered riding with him another day when he accidentally drove past a stop sign. A policeman pulled up to the car and said:

"All right, boy, pull over and let me see your license."

My father replied indignantly, "I'm no boy." Then, pointing to me, "This is a boy. I'm a man, and until you call me one, I will not listen to you."

The policeman was so shocked that he wrote the ticket up nervously, and left the scene as quickly as possible.

From before I was born, my father had refused to ride the city buses, after witnessing a brutal attack on a load of Negro passengers. He had led the fight in Atlanta to equalize teachers' salaries, and had been instrumental in the elimination of Jim Crow elevators in the courthouse. As pastor of the Ebenezer Baptist Church, where he still presides over a congregation of four thousand, he had wielded great influence in the Negro community, and had perhaps won the grudging respect of the whites. At any rate, they had never attacked him physically, a fact that filled my brother and sister and me with wonder as we grew up in this tension-packed atmosphere.

With this heritage, it is not surprising that I had also learned to abhor segregation, considering it both rationally inexplicable and morally unjustifiable. As a teenager I had never been able to accept the fact of having to go to the back of a bus or sit in the segregated section of a train. The first time that I had been seated behind a curtain in a dining car, I felt as if the curtain had been dropped on my selfhood. Having the usual growing boy's pleasure in movies, I had yet gone to a downtown theater in Atlanta only once. The experience of having to enter a rear door and sit in a filthy peanut gallery was so obnoxious that I could not enjoy the picture. I could never adjust to the separate waiting rooms, separate eating places, separate rest rooms, partly because the separate was always unequal, and partly because the very idea of separation did something to my sense of dignity and self-respect.

Now, I thought, as the plane carried me toward Detroit, I have a chance to escape from the long night of segregation. Can I return to a society that condones a system I have abhorred since childhood?

These questions were still unanswered when I returned to Boston. I discussed them with my wife, Coretta (we had been married less than a year), to find that she too was hesitant about returning South. We discussed the all-important question of raising children in the bonds of segregation. We reviewed our own growth in the South, and the many advantages that we had been deprived of as a result of segregation. The question of my wife's musical career came up. She was certain that a Northern city would afford a greater opportunity for continued study than any city in the deep South. For several days we talked and thought and prayed over each of these matters. Finally we agreed that, in spite of the disadvantages and inevitable sacrifices, our greatest service could be rendered in our native South. We came to the conclusion that we had something of a moral obligation to return—at least for a few years.

The South, after all, was our home. Despite its shortcomings we loved it as home, and had a real desire to do something about the problems that we had felt so keenly as youngsters. We never wanted to be considered detached spectators. Since racial discrimination was most intense in the South, we felt that some of the Negroes who had received a portion of their training in other sections of the country should return to share their broader contacts and educational experience in its solution. Moreover, despite having to sacrifice much of the cultural life we loved, despite the existence of Jim Crow which kept reminding us at all times of the color of our skin, we had the feeling that something remarkable was unfolding in the South, and we wanted to be on hand to witness it. The region had marvelous possibilities, and once it came to itself and removed the blight of racial segregation, it would experience a moral, political, and economic boom hardly paralleled by any other section of the country.

With this decision my inclination toward the pastorate temporarily won out over my desire to teach, and I decided to accept the call to Dexter for a few years and satisfy my fondness for scholarship later by turning to the teaching field. I sent a telegram to Montgomery that I would be down in three weeks to discuss details.

So I went back to Montgomery. After exploring arrangements with the officers, I accepted the pastorate. Because of my desire to spend at least four more months of intensive work on my doctoral thesis, I asked for and was granted the condition that I would not be required to take up the full-time pastorate until September 1, 1954. I agreed, however, to come down to Montgomery at least once a month to keep things running smoothly during this interim period. On a Sunday in May 1954 I preached my first sermon as minister of the Dexter Avenue Baptist Church, and for the next four months I commuted by plane between Boston and Montgomery.

On my July trip I was accompanied by Coretta. Montgomery was not unfamiliar to her, for her home was just 80 miles away, in the little town of Marion, Alabama. There her father, Obie Scott, though born on a farm, had made a success in business, operating a trucking concern, a combination filling station and grocery store, and a chicken farm. Despite the reprisals and physical threats of his white competitors, he had dared to make a decent living for his family, and to maintain an abiding faith in the future. Coretta had lived in Marion until she left to attend Antioch College in Yellow Springs, Ohio. Having inherited a talent for music from her mother, Bernice Scott, as well as the strength of quiet determination, she had then gone on with the aid of a scholarship to work her way through the New England Conservatory in Boston. It was in Boston that I had met and fallen in love with the attractive young singer whose gentle manner and air of repose did not disguise her lively spirit. And although we had returned to Marion on June 18, 1953, to be married by my father on the Scotts' spacious lawn, it was in Boston that we had begun our married life together.

So on the July visit Coretta looked at Montgomery with fresh eyes. Since her teens she had breathed the free air of unsegregated colleges, and stayed as a welcome guest in white homes. Now in preparation for our long-term return to the South, she visited the Negro section of town where we would be living without choice. She saw the Negroes crowded into the backs of segregated buses and knew that she would be riding there too. But on the same visit she was introduced to the church and cordially received by its fine congregation. And with her sense of optimism and balance, which were to be my constant support in the days to come, she placed her faith on the side of the opportunities and the challenge for Christian service that were offered by Dexter and the Montgomery community.

On September 1, 1954, we moved into the parsonage and I began my full-time pastorate. The first months were busy with the usual chores of getting to know a new house, a new job, a new city. There were old friendships to pick up and new ones to be made, and little time to look beyond our private lives to the general community around us. And although we had come back to the South with the hope of playing a part in the changes we knew were on the horizon, we had no notion yet of how the changes would come about, and no inkling that in little more than a year we would be involved in a movement that was to alter Montgomery forever and to have repercussions throughout the world.

II

Montgomery Before the Protest

The church work was stimulating from the beginning. The first few weeks in the autumn of 1954 were spent formulating a program that would be meaningful to this particular congregation. I was anxious to change the impression in the community that Dexter was a sort of silk-stocking church catering only to a certain class. Often it was referred to as the "big folks' church." Revolting against this idea, I was convinced that worship at its best is a social experience with people of all levels of life coming together to realize their oneness and unity under God. Whenever the church, consciously or unconsciously, caters to one class it loses the spiritual force of the "whosoever will, let him come" doctrine, and is in danger of becoming little more than a social club with a thin veneer of religiosity.

I was also concerned with broadening the auxiliary program of the church. These activities, when I arrived, consisted chiefly of the Sunday School, where adults and children assembled to study the tenets of Christianity and the Bible; the Baptist Training Union, designed to develop Christian leadership; and the Missionary Society, which carried the message of the church into the community. Among the new functions I decided to recommend were a committee to revitalize religious education; a social service committee to channel and invigorate services to the sick and needy; a social and political action committee; a committee to raise and administer scholarship funds for high school graduates; and a cultural committee to give encouragement to promising artists.

Since many points in the new program represented a definite departure from the traditional way of doing things, I was somewhat dubious about its acceptance. I therefore presented my recommendations to the church with some trepidation; but, to my surprise, they were heartily approved. The response and coöperation of the members from this moment on was impressive. Almost immediately the membership began to grow, and the financial report for the first six months revealed that the income of the church had almost tripled over previous years. The various new committees were functioning well, and the program of religious education was characterized by sturdy growth.

For several months I had to divide my efforts between completing my thesis and carrying out my duties with the church. I rose every morning at five-thirty and spent three hours writing the thesis, returning to it late at night for another three hours. The remainder of the day was given to church work, including, besides the weekly service, marriages, funerals, and personal conferences. One day each week was given over to visiting and praying with members who were either sick or otherwise confined to their homes.

A great deal of time in the early days was also occupied with getting to know all the members of the congregation. This entailed visiting them at home and attending the various auxiliary meetings of the church. Almost every week I attended from five to ten such group meetings, and most of my early evenings were consumed in this fashion. I was also spending a minimum of fifteen hours a week in preparing my Sunday sermon. I usually began an outline on Tuesday. On Wednesday I did the necessary research and thought of illustrative material and life situations that would give the sermon practical content. On Friday I began writing, and usually finished the writing on Saturday night.

I still found additional time to take an immediate interest in the larger community of Montgomery. The city's economic life was heavily influenced by the presence there of the Maxwell and Gunter Air Force bases. According to the annual report of the Montgomery Chamber of Commerce, these two bases channeled a total of $58 million into Montgomery's business economy during 1955. One in every fourteen employed civilians in Montgomery worked at these bases, and approximately one in every seven families was an air force family, either civilian or military. Four thousand families living outside base reservations occupied homes in the city. Yet ironically, although the bases, which contributed so much to the economic life of the community, were fully integrated, the city around them adhered to a rigorous pattern of racial segregation. One could not help wishing that the vast economic power of the federal agencies were being used for the good of race relations in Montgomery.

Modern Montgomery is a prominent market for cotton, livestock, yellow pine, and hardwood lumber, and is one of the nation's important centers for the manufacture of commercial fertilizer. It has the largest cattle market east of Fort Worth, Texas, and south of the Ohio River, marketing approximately $30 million worth of cattle annually. But there is a dearth of heavy industry. This lack of industry is one of the reasons why so many Negroes go into domestic service: 63 per cent of the Negro women workers in Montgomery are domestics, and 48 per cent of the Negro men are laborers or domestic workers. It is also probably one of the factors in the appalling gap between the living conditions of the whites and the Negroes. In 1950 the median income for the approximately 70,000 white people of

Montgomery was $1730, compared with $970 for the 50,000 Negroes. Ninty-four per cent of the white families in Montgomery
have flush toilets inside their homes, while only 31 per cent of the
Negro families enjoy such facilities. Aside, then, from the problem
of segregation itself, with its effects on every aspect of Negro
life, it was clear that Montgomery's Negroes were also the victims
of severe economic deprivation.

The two communities moved, as it were, along separate channels. The schools of course were segregated; and the United
States Supreme Court decision on school integration, handed
down in May 1954, appeared to have no effect on Montgomery's
determination to keep them that way. If a white man and a Negro
wanted to ride in a taxi together, they could not have done so,
since by law white operators served white passengers exclusively
and Negroes rode in a separate system confined to them. True,
Negroes and whites met as employers and employees, and they
rode to work together at either ends of the same buses, with
a sharp line of separation between the two groups. They used the
same shopping centers, though Negroes were sometimes forced
to wait until all the whites had been served, and they were
seldom given the dignity of courtesy titles. In several sections of
town, Negro and white residential neighborhoods adjoined, and
in others they interlocked like the fingers of two hands. But each
section turned its back on its neighbor and faced into its own
community for its social and cultural life.

There were no integrated professional organizations of physicians, lawyers, teachers, and so forth; and even when such professionals shared membership in national organizations, they went
their separate ways at home. No interracial ministerial alliance
existed in Montgomery. There was no local Urban League to
bring Negro and white together on an interracial board, and the

active membership of the Montgomery Chapter of the National Association for the Advancement of Colored People (NAACP) was entirely Negro. The largest institution of higher learning in Montgomery was the all-Negro Alabama State College, mainly devoted to teacher training, with a faculty of almost 200 and a student body of approximately 2000. Although the faculty had included such nationally known figures as Horace Mann Bond and Charles H. Thompson, and the college still exerted a lively cultural influence on both city and state, it drew few local white visitors to its handsome campus. In fact, the local chapter of the Alabama Council on Human Relations alone in Montgomery brought the two races together in mutual efforts to solve shared problems.

Alabama law and its administration had worked to keep Negro voting down to a minimum. By 1940 there were not more than 2000 Negro voters in all Alabama. Today the number is closer to 50,000, but although this represents progress, it is still less than 10 per cent of all Negroes of voting age in the state. In 1954 there were some 30,000 Negroes of voting age in Montgomery County, but only a few more than 2000 were registered. This low figure was in part the result of the Negroes' own lack of interest or persistence in surmounting the barriers erected against them; but the barriers were themselves formidable. Alabama law gives the registrars wide discretionary powers. At the registration office are separate lines and separate tables for voters according to race. The registrars servicing Negro lines move at a noticeably leisurely pace, so that of fifty Negroes in line, as few as fifteen may be reached by the end of the day. All voters are required to fill out a long questionnaire as a test of eligibility. Often Negroes fill out the questionnaire at several different times before they have been informed that they have done so successfully. In the light of these facts it was not surprising to find that there was no Negro in public office in either the city or the county of Montgomery.

As an expression of my concern with such problems as these, one of the first committees that I set up in my church was designed to keep the congregation intelligently informed on the social, political, and economic situations. The duties of the Social and Political Action Committee were, among others, to keep before the congregation the importance of the NAACP and the necessity of being registered voters, and—during state and national elections—to sponsor forums and mass meetings to discuss the major issues. I sought members for this committee who had already evinced an interest in social problems, and who had some prior experience in this area. Fortunately this was not a difficult task, for Dexter had several members who were deeply concerned with community problems, and who accepted with alacrity. Interestingly enough, two members of this committee—Mrs. Jo Ann Robinson and Rufus Lewis—were among the first people to become prominent in the bus boycott that was soon to mobilize the latent strength of Montgomery's Negro community.

As the year passed I saw impressive results from the work of this committee. By the first of November it was publishing a biweekly newsletter, SAPAC, which was distributed to every member of the church and proved to be of great value in placing major social and political issues before the church members. Under the committee's auspices a voting clinic had trained almost every unregistered member of the congregation in the pitfalls of discriminatory registration procedures. By November 1955, in my annual report to the membership, I was able to say that "the work of this committee has been superb, and every member of Dexter has felt its influence. Through the work of this committee many persons have become registered voters, and Dexter has led all other churches in Montgomery in contributions to the NAACP."

After having started the program of the church on its way, I joined the local branch of the NAACP and began to take an active interest in implementing its program in the community itself. Besides raising money through my church, I made several speeches for the NAACP in Montgomery and elsewhere. Less than a year after I joined the branch I was elected to the executive committee. By attending most of the monthly meetings I was brought face to face with some of the racial problems that plagued the community, especially those involving the courts.

Before my arrival in Montgomery, and for several years after, most of the local NAACP's energies and funds were devoted to the defense of Jeremiah Reeves. Reeves, a drummer in a Negro band, had been arrested at the age of sixteen, accused of raping a white woman. One of the authorities had led him to the death chamber, threatening that if he did not confess at once he would burn there later. His confession, extracted under this duress, was later retracted, and for the remaining seven years that his case, and his life, dragged on, he continued to deny not only the charge of rape but the accusation of having had sexual relations at all with his white accuser.

The NAACP hired the lawyers and raised the money for Reeves's defense. In the local court he was found guilty and condemned to death. The conviction was upheld in a series of appeals through the Alabama courts. The case was appealed to the United States Supreme Court on two occasions. The first time, the Court reversed the decision and turned it back to the State Supreme Court for rehearing. The second time, the United States Supreme Court agreed to hear the case but later dismissed it, thus leaving the Alabama Court free to electrocute. After the failure of a final appeal to the Governor to commute the sentence, the police officials kept their promise. On March 28, 1958, Reeves was electrocuted.

The Reeves case was typical of the unequal justice of Southern courts. In the years that he sat in jail, several white men in Alabama had also been charged with rape; but their accusers were Negro girls. They were seldom arrested; if arrested, they were soon released by the Grand Jury; none was ever brought to trial. For good reason the Negroes of the South had learned to fear and mistrust the white man's justice.

Around the time that I started working with the NAACP the Alabama Council on Human Relations also caught my attention. This interracial group was concerned with human relations in the State of Alabama and employed educational methods to achieve its purpose. An affiliate of the Southern Regional Council, and the successor to the Alabama Inter-Racial Committee, the Council on Human Relations sought to attain through research and action equal opportunity for all the people of Alabama. Its basic philosophy recognized "that all men are created equal under God. Interpreted into the life of our nation, this means that each individual is endowed with the right of equal opportunity to contribute to and share in the life of our nation. No individual or group of individuals has the privilege to limit this right in any way."

I joined this organization, and attended most of the monthly meetings of the Montgomery Chapter, which were held in the meeting room of my church. After working with the Council for a few months I was elected to the office of vice-president, and served in this capacity until other responsibilities intervened. The president of the Council was Rev. Ray Wadley, the young white minister of St. Mark's Methodist Church. A native Southerner, he

was later shifted to a small, backwoods community after his congregation protested his activities in the field of race relations.
Two other prominent white members of the Council were Revs.
Thomas P. Thrasher and Robert Graetz, both of whom were to be
prominent in the subsequent bus struggle.

Although the Montgomery Council never had a large membership, it played an important role. As the only truly interracial
group in Montgomery, it served to keep the desperately needed
channels of communication open between the races. Men often
hate each other because they fear each other; they fear each other
because they do not know each other; they do not know each
other because they cannot communicate; they cannot communicate because they are separated. In providing an avenue of communication, the Council was fulfilling a necessary condition for
better race relations in the South.

I was surprised to learn that many people found my dual interest in the NAACP and the Council inconsistent. Many Negroes
felt that integration could come only through legislation and court
action—the chief emphases of the NAACP. Many white people
felt that integration could come only through education—the
chief emphasis of the Council on Human Relations. How could
one give his allegiance to two organizations whose approaches
and methods seemed so diametrically opposed?

This question betrayed an assumption that there was only one
approach to the solution of the race problem. On the contrary I
felt that both approaches were necessary. Through education we
seek to change attitudes; through legislation and court orders
we seek to regulate behavior. Through education we seek to
change internal feelings (prejudice, hate, etc.); through legislation and court orders we seek to control the external effects of
those feelings. Through education we seek to break down the
spiritual barriers to integration; through legislation and court

orders we seek to break down the physical barriers to integration. One method is not a substitute for the other, but a meaningful and necessary supplement. Anyone who starts out with the conviction that the road to racial justice is only one lane wide will inevitably create a traffic jam and make the journey infinitely longer. My work with the NAACP and the Alabama Council on Human Relations grew out of the conviction that both organizations met a real need in the community, and each carried out its work at a high level of dignity and wisdom.

As time went on, I discovered several things in the Negro community which needed to be remedied before any real social progress could be effected. First, there was an appalling lack of unity among the leaders. Several civic groups existed, each at loggerheads with the other. There was the organization known as the Progressive Democrats headed by E. D. Nixon. There was the Citizens Committee headed by Rufus Lewis. There was the Women's Political Council headed by Mrs. Mary Fair Burks and Jo Ann Robinson. There was the NAACP headed by R. L. Matthews. Smaller groups further divided the Negro community. While the heads of each of these organizations were able and dedicated leaders with common aims, their separate allegiances made it difficult for them to come together on the basis of a higher unity.

Many people sensed the effects of this crippling factionalism. Early in 1955 some influential leaders attempted to solve the problem by organizing a group which finally came to be known as the Citizens Coördinating Committee. I can remember the anticipation with which I attended the first meeting of this group, feeling that here the Negro community had an answer to a problem that had stood too long as a stumbling block to social progress. Soon, however, my hopes were shattered. Due to a lack of tenacity on the part of the leaders and of active interest on the part of the citizens in general, the Citizens Coördinating Committee finally dissolved. With the breakdown of this promising undertaking, it appeared that the tragic division in the Negro community could be cured only by some divine miracle.

But not only was the community faced with competing leadership; it was also crippled by the indifference of the educated group. This indifference expressed itself in a lack of participation in any move toward better racial conditions, and a sort of tacit acceptance of things as they were. To be sure, there were always some educated people who stood in the forefront of the struggle for racial justice—but they were exceptions. The vast majority were indifferent and complacent.

Some of this lack of concern had its basis in fear. Many of the educated group were employed in vulnerable positions, and a forthright stand in the area of racial justice might result in the loss of a job. So rather than jeopardize their economic security, many steered clear of any move toward altering the status quo. This, however, was not the whole story. Too much of the inaction was due to sheer apathy. Even in areas—such as voting—where they would not really be accused of tampering with the established order, the educated group had an indifference that for a period appeared incurable.

The apparent apathy of the Negro ministers presented a special problem. A faithful few had always shown a deep concern for social problems, but too many had remained aloof from the area of social responsibility. Much of this indifference, it is true, stemmed from a sincere feeling that ministers were not supposed to get mixed up in such earthly, temporal matters as social and economic improvement; they were to "preach the gospel," and keep men's minds centered on "the heavenly." But however sincere, this view of religion, I felt, was too confined.

Certainly, otherworldly concerns have a deep and significant place in all religions worthy of the name. Any religion that is completely earthbound sells its birthright for a mess of naturalistic pottage. Religion, at its best, deals not only with man's preliminary concerns but with his inescapable ultimate concern. When religion overlooks this basic fact it is reduced to a mere ethical system in which eternity is absorbed into time and God is relegated to a sort of meaningless figment of the human imagination.

But a religion true to its nature must also be concerned about man's social conditions. Religion deals with both earth and heaven, both time and eternity. Religion operates not only on the vertical plane but also on the horizontal. It seeks not only to integrate men with God but to integrate men with men and each man with himself. This means, at bottom, that the Christian gospel is a two-way road. On the one hand it seeks to change the souls of men, and thereby unite them with God; on the other hand it seeks to change the environmental conditions of men so that the soul will have a chance after it is changed. Any religion that professes to be concerned with the souls of men and is not concerned with the slums that damn them, the economic conditions that strangle them, and the social conditions that cripple them is a dry-as-dust religion. Such a religion is the kind the Marxists like to see—an opiate of the people.

Another striking fact about Montgomery's Negro community was the apparent passivity of the majority of the uneducated. While there were always some who struck out against segregation, the largest number accepted it without apparent protest. Not only did they seem resigned to segregation per se; they also accepted the abuses and indignities which came with it. My predecessor at the Dexter Avenue Baptist Church—Rev. Vernon Johns—tells of an incident that illustrates the attitude of the people at this time. One day he boarded a bus and sat in one of the front seats reserved for whites only. The bus driver demanded that he move back. Mr. Johns refused. The operator then ordered him off the bus. Again Mr. Johns refused, until the driver agreed to return his fare. Before leaving, Mr. Johns stood in the aisle and asked how many of his people would follow him off the bus in protest. Not a single person responded. A few days later when he chided a woman who had been on the bus for not joining his protest, she quoted her fellow passengers as saying: "You ought to knowed better."

Some of the passivity of the uneducated could, like that of the educated, be attributed to the fear of economic reprisals. Dependent on the white community, they dared not protest against unjust racial conditions for fear of losing their jobs. But perhaps an even more basic force at work was their corroding sense of inferiority, which often expressed itself in a lack of self-respect. Many unconsciously wondered whether they actually deserved any better conditions. Their minds and souls were so conditioned to the system of segregation that they submissively adjusted themselves to things as they were. This is the ultimate tragedy of segregation. It not only harms one physically but injures one spiritually. It scars the soul and degrades the personality. It inflicts the segregated with a false sense of inferiority, while confirming the segregator in a false estimate of his own superiority. It is a system which forever stares the segregated in the face, saying: "You are less than . . ." "You are not equal to . . ." The system of segregation itself was responsible for much of the passivity of the Negroes of Montgomery.

So I found the Negro community the victim of a threefold malady—factionalism among the leaders, indifference in the educated group, and passivity in the uneducated. All of these conditions had almost persuaded me that no lasting social reform could ever be achieved in Montgomery.

Beneath the surface, however, there was a ground swell of discontent. Such men as Vernon Johns and E. D. Nixon had never tired of keeping the problem before the conscience of the community. When others had feared to speak, they had spoken with courage. When others had dared not take a stand, they had stood with valor and determination.

Vernon Johns, now the director of Maryland State Baptist Center, was a brilliant preacher with a creative mind and an incredibly retentive memory. It was not unusual for him to quote from the classics of literature and philosophy for hours without ever referring to a manuscript. A fearless man, he never allowed an injustice to come to his attention without speaking out against it. When he was still pastor, hardly a Sunday passed that he did not lash out against complacency. He often chided the congregation for sitting up so proudly with their many academic degrees, and yet lacking the very thing that degrees should confer, that is, self-respect. One of his basic theses was that any individual who submitted willingly to injustice did not really deserve more justice.

Johns loved to farm and live close to nature. He agreed with Booker T. Washington that "no race can prosper till it learns there is as much dignity in tilling a field as in writing a poem." Johns also felt, as Washington did, that the Negro must lift himself by his own bootstraps, and that one of the best ways to do this was by gaining an economic stronghold. Considering it a tragedy that the Negro produced so little of what he consumed, he consistently urged the Negroes of Montgomery to pool their economic resources. As a result, a few enterprising individuals came together in 1953, under Johns's influence, and organized Farm and City Enterprises—a coöperative supermarket which has today developed into a thriving business. This was a *tour de force* in a community that had generally been abysmally slow to move.

Like Vernon Johns, E. D. Nixon had always been a foe of injustice. You could look at the face of this tall, dark-skinned, graying man and tell that he was a fighter. In his work as a Pullman porter—a job he still holds—he was in close contact with organized labor. He had served as state president of the NAACP and also as president of the Montgomery branch. Through each of these mediums E. D. Nixon worked fearlessly to achieve the rights of his people, and to rouse the Negroes from their apathy. Thanks to his efforts, hundreds of Negroes had been encouraged to register at the polls. As the result of his fearless stand, he was one of the chief voices of the Negro community in the area of civil rights, a symbol of the hopes and aspirations of the long oppressed people of the State of Alabama.

So through the work of men like Johns and Nixon there had developed beneath the surface a slow fire of discontent, fed by the continuing indignities and inequities to which the Negroes were subjected. These were the fearless men who created the atmosphere for the social revolution that was slowly developing in the Cradle of the Confederacy.

But this discontent was still latent in 1954. At that time both Negroes and whites accepted the well-established patterns of segregation as a matter of fact. Hardly anyone challenged the system. Montgomery was an easygoing town; it could even have been described as a peaceful town. But the peace was achieved at the cost of human servitude.

Many months later, an influential white citizen of Montgomery was to protest to me:

"Over the years we have had such peaceful and harmonious race relations here. Why have you and your associates come in to destroy this long tradition?"

My reply was simple: "Sir," I said, "you have never had real peace in Montgomery. You have had a sort of negative peace in which the Negro too often accepted his state of subordination. But this is not true peace. True peace is not merely the absence of tension; it is the presence of justice. The tension we see in Montgomery today is the necessary tension that comes when the oppressed rise up and start to move forward toward a permanent, positive peace."

I went on to speculate that this was what Jesus meant when he said: "I have not come to bring peace, but a sword." Certainly Jesus did not mean that he came to bring a physical sword. He seems to have been saying in substance: "I have not come to bring this old negative peace with its deadening passivity. I have come to lash out against such a peace. Whenever I come, a conflict is precipitated between the old and the new. Whenever I come, a division sets in between justice and injustice. I have come to bring a positive peace which is the presence of justice, love, yea, even the Kingdom of God."

The racial peace which had existed in Montgomery was not a Christian peace. It was a pagan peace and it had been bought at too great a price.

One place where the peace had long been precarious was on the city-wide buses. Here the Negro was daily reminded of the indignities of segregation. There were no Negro drivers, and although some of the white men who drove the buses were courteous, all too many were abusive and vituperative. It was not uncommon to hear them referring to Negro passengers as "niggers," "black cows," and "black apes." Frequently Negroes paid their fares at the front door, and then were forced to get off and reboard the bus at the rear. Often the bus pulled off with the

Negro's dime in the box before he had had time to reach the rear door.

An even more humiliating practice was the custom of forcing Negroes to stand over empty seats reserved for "whites only." Even if the bus had no white passengers, and Negroes were packed throughout, they were prohibited from sitting in the first four seats (which held ten persons). But the practice went further. If white passengers were already occupying all of their reserved seats and additional white people boarded the bus, Negroes sitting in the unreserved section immediately behind the whites were asked to stand so that the whites could be seated. If the Negroes refused to stand and move back, they were arrested. In most instances the Negroes submitted without protest. Occasionally, however, there were those, like Vernon Johns, who refused.

A few months after my arrival a fifteen-year-old high school girl, Claudette Colvin, was pulled off a bus, handcuffed, and taken to jail because she refused to give up her seat for a white passenger. This atrocity seemed to arouse the Negro community. There was talk of boycotting the buses in protest. A citizens committee was formed to talk with the manager of the bus company and the City Commission, demanding a statement of policy on seating and more courtesy from the drivers.

I was asked to serve on this committee. We met one afternoon in March 1955 in the office of J. E. Bagley, manager of the Montgomery City Lines. Dave Birmingham, the police commissioner at the time, represented the city commission. Both men were quite pleasant, and expressed deep concern over what had happened. Bagley went so far as to admit that the bus operator was wrong in having Miss Colvin arrested, and promised to reprimand him. Commissioner Birmingham agreed to have the city attorney give a definite statement on the seating policy of the city. We left the meeting hopeful; but nothing happened. The same old patterns of humiliation continued. The city attorney never clarified the law. Claudette Colvin was convicted with a suspended sentence.

But despite the fact that the city commission and the bus company did not act, something else had begun to happen. The long repressed feelings of resentment on the part of the Negroes had begun to stir. The fear and apathy which had for so long cast a shadow on the life of the Negro community were gradually fading before a new spirit of courage and self-respect. The inaction of the city and bus officials after the Colvin case would make it necessary for them in a few months to meet another committee, infinitely more determined. Next time they would face a committee supported by the longings and aspirations of nearly 50,000 people, tired people who had come to see that it is ultimately more honorable to walk the streets in dignity than to ride the buses in humiliation.

III

The Decisive Arrest

On December 1, 1955, an attractive Negro seamstress, Mrs. Rosa Parks, boarded the Cleveland Avenue Bus in downtown Montgomery. She was returning home after her regular day's work in the Montgomery Fair—a leading department store. Tired from long hours on her feet, Mrs. Parks sat down in the first seat behind the section reserved for whites. Not long after she took her seat, the bus operator ordered her, along with three other Negro passengers, to move back in order to accommodate boarding white passengers. By this time every seat in the bus was taken. This meant that if Mrs. Parks followed the driver's command she would have to stand while a white male passenger, who had just boarded the bus, would sit. The other three Negro passengers immediately complied with the driver's request. But Mrs. Parks quietly refused. The result was her arrest.

There was to be much speculation about why Mrs. Parks did not obey the driver. Many people in the white community argued that she had been "planted" by the NAACP in order to lay the groundwork for a test case, and at first glance that explanation seemed plausible, since she was a former secretary of the local branch of the NAACP. So persistent and persuasive was this argument that it convinced many reporters from all over the country. Later on, when I was having press conferences three times a week—in order to accommodate the reporters and journalists who came to Montgomery from all over the world—the invariable first question was: "Did the NAACP start the bus boycott?"

But the accusation was totally unwarranted, as the testimony of both Mrs. Parks and the officials of the NAACP revealed. Actually, no one can understand the action of Mrs. Parks unless he realizes that eventually the cup of endurance runs over, and the human personality cries out, "I can take it no longer." Mrs. Parks's refusal to move back was her intrepid affirmation that she had had enough. It was an individual expression of a timeless longing for human dignity and freedom. She was not "planted" there by the NAACP, or any other organization; she was planted there by her personal sense of dignity and self-respect. She was anchored to that seat by the accumulated indignities of days gone by and the boundless aspirations of generations yet unborn. She was a victim of both the forces of history and the forces of destiny. She had been tracked down by the *Zeitgeist*—the spirit of the time.

Fortunately, Mrs. Parks was ideal for the role assigned to her by history. She was a charming person with a radiant personality, soft spoken and calm in all situations. Her character was impeccable and her dedication deep-rooted. All of these traits together made her one of the most respected people in the Negro community.

Only E. D. Nixon—the signer of Mrs. Parks's bond—and one or two other persons were aware of the arrest when it occurred early Thursday evening. Later in the evening the word got around to a few influential women of the community, mostly members of the Women's Political Council. After a series of telephone calls back and forth they agreed that the Negroes should boycott the buses. They immediately suggested the idea to Nixon, and he readily concurred. In his usual courageous manner he agreed to spearhead the idea.

Early Friday morning, December 2, Nixon called me. He was so caught up in what he was about to say that he forgot to greet me with the usual "hello" but plunged immediately into the story of what had happened to Mrs. Parks the night before. I listened, deeply shocked, as he described the humiliating incident. "We have taken this type of thing too long already," Nixon concluded, his voice trembling. "I feel that the time has come to boycott the buses. Only through a boycott can we make it clear to the white folks that we will not accept this type of treatment any longer."

I agreed at once that some protest was necessary, and that the boycott method would be an effective one.

Just before calling me Nixon had discussed the idea with Rev. Ralph Abernathy, the young minister of Montgomery's First Baptist Church who was to become one of the central figures in the protest, and one of my closest associates. Abernathy also felt a bus boycott was our best course of action. So for thirty or forty minutes the three of us telephoned back and forth concerning plans and strategy. Nixon suggested that we call a meeting of all the ministers and civic leaders the same evening in order to get their thinking on the proposal, and I offered my church as the meeting place. The three of us got busy immediately. With the sanction of Rev. H. H. Hubbard—president of the Baptist Ministerial Alliance—Abernathy and I began calling all of the Baptist ministers. Since most of the Methodist ministers were attending a denominational meeting in one of the local churches that afternoon, it was possible for Abernathy to get the announcement to all of them simultaneously. Nixon reached Mrs. A. W. West—the widow of a prominent dentist—and enlisted her assistance in getting word to the civic leaders.

By early afternoon the arrest of Mrs. Parks was becoming public knowledge. Word of it spread around the community like uncontrolled fire. Telephones began to ring in almost rhythmic succession. By two o'clock an enthusiastic group had mimeographed leaflets concerning the arrest and the proposed boycott, and by evening these had been widely circulated.

As the hour for the evening meeting arrived, I approached the doors of the church with some apprehension, wondering how many of the leaders would respond to our call. Fortunately, it was one of those pleasant winter nights of unseasonable warmth, and to our relief, almost everybody who had been invited was on hand. More than forty people, from every segment of Negro life, were crowded into the large church meeting room. I saw physicians, schoolteachers, lawyers, businessmen, postal workers, union leaders, and clergymen. Virtually every organization of the Negro community was represented.

The largest number there was from the Christian ministry. Having left so many civic meetings in the past sadly disappointed by the dearth of ministers participating, I was filled with joy when I entered the church and found so many of them there; for then I knew that something unusual was about to happen.

Had E. D. Nixon been present, he would probably have been automatically selected to preside, but he had had to leave town earlier in the afternoon for his regular run on the railroad. In his absence, we concluded that Rev. L. Roy Bennett—as president of the Interdenominational Ministerial Alliance—was the logical person to take the chair. He agreed and was seated, his tall, erect figure dominating the room.

The meeting opened around seven-thirty with H. H. Hubbard leading a brief devotional period. Then Bennett moved into action, explaining the purpose of the gathering. With excited gestures he reported on Mrs. Parks's resistance and her arrest. He presented the proposal that the Negro citizens of Montgomery should boycott the buses on Monday in protest. "Now is the time to move," he concluded. "This is no time to talk; it is time to act."

So seriously did Bennett take his "no time to talk" admonition that for quite a while he refused to allow anyone to make a suggestion or even raise a question, insisting that we should move on and appoint committees to implement the proposal. This approach aroused the opposition of most of those present, and created a temporary uproar. For almost forty-five minutes the confusion persisted. Voices rose high, and many people threatened to leave if they could not raise questions and offer suggestions. It looked for a time as though the movement had come to an end before it began. But finally, in the face of this blistering protest, Bennett agreed to open the meeting to discussion.

Immediately questions began to spring up from the floor. Several people wanted further clarification of Mrs. Parks's actions and arrest. Then came the more practical questions. How long would the protest last? How would the idea be further disseminated throughout the community? How would the people be transported to and from their jobs?

As we listened to the lively discussion, we were heartened to notice that, despite the lack of coherence in the meeting, not once did anyone question the validity or desirability of the boycott itself. It seemed to be the unanimous sense of the group that the boycott should take place.

The ministers endorsed the plan with enthusiasm, and promised to go to their congregations on Sunday morning and drive home their approval of the projected one-day protest. Their co-öperation was significant, since virtually all of the influential Negro ministers of the city were present. It was decided that we should hold a city-wide mass meeting on Monday night, December 5, to determine how long we would abstain from riding the buses. Rev. A. W. Wilson—minister of the Holt Street Baptist Church— offered his church, which was ideal as a meeting place because of its size and central location. The group agreed that additional leaflets should be distributed on Saturday, and the chairman appointed a committee, including myself, to prepare the statement.

Our committee went to work while the meeting was still in progress. The final message was shorter than the one that had appeared on the first leaflets, but the substance was the same. It read as follows:

> Don't ride the bus to work, to town, to school, or any place Monday, December 5.
>
> Another Negro woman has been arrested and put in jail because she refused to give up her bus seat.
>
> Don't ride the buses to work, to town, to school, or anywhere on Monday. If you work, take a cab, or share a ride, or walk.
>
> Come to a mass meeting, Monday at 7:00 P.M., at the Holt Street Baptist Church for further instruction.

After finishing the statement the committee began to mimeograph it on the church machine; but since it was late, I volunteered to have the job completed early Saturday morning.

The final question before the meeting concerned transportation. It was agreed that we should try to get the Negro taxi companies of the city—eighteen in number, with approximately 210 taxis—to transport the people for the same price that they were currently paying on the bus. A committee was appointed to make this contact, with Rev. W. J. Powell, minister of the Old Ship A.M.E. Zion Church, as chairman.

With these responsibilities before us the meeting closed. We left with our hearts caught up in a great idea. The hours were moving fast. The clock on the wall read almost midnight, but the clock in our souls revealed that it was daybreak.

I was so excited that I slept very little that night, and early the next morning I was on my way to the church to get the leaflets out. By nine o'clock the church secretary had finished mimeographing the 7000 leaflets and by eleven o'clock an army of women and young people had taken them off to distribute by hand.

Those on the committee that was to contact the taxi companies got to work early Saturday afternoon. They worked assiduously, and by evening they had reached practically all of the companies, and triumphantly reported that every one of them so far had agreed to coöperate with the proposed boycott by transporting the passengers to and from work for the regular ten-cent bus fare.

Meanwhile our efforts to get the word across to the Negro community were abetted in an unexpected way. A maid who could not read very well came into possession of one of the unsigned appeals that had been distributed Friday afternoon. Apparently not knowing what the leaflet said, she gave it to her employer. As soon as the white employer received the notice she turned it over to the local newspaper, and the *Montgomery Advertiser* made the contents of the leaflet a front-page story on Saturday morning. It appears that the *Advertiser* printed the story in order to let the white community know what the Negroes were up to; but the whole thing turned out to the Negroes' advantage, since it served to bring the information to hundreds who had not previously heard of the plan. By Sunday afternoon word had spread to practically every Negro citizen of Montgomery. Only a few people who lived in remote areas had not heard of it.

After a heavy day of work, I went home late Sunday afternoon and sat down to read the morning paper. There was a long article on the proposed boycott. Implicit throughout the article, I noticed, was the idea that the Negroes were preparing to use the same approach to their problem as the White Citizens Councils used. This suggested parallel had serious implications. The White Citizens Councils, which had had their birth in Mississippi a few months after the Supreme Court's school decision, had come into being to preserve segregation. The Councils had multiplied rapidly throughout the South, purporting to achieve their ends by the legal maneuvers of "interposition" and "nullification." Unfortunately, however, the actions of some of these Councils extended far beyond the bounds of the law. Their methods were the methods of open and covert terror, brutal intimidation, and threats of starvation to Negro men, women, and children. They took open economic reprisals against whites who dared to protest their defiance of the law, and the aim of their boycotts was not merely to impress their victims but to destroy them if possible.

Disturbed by the fact that our pending action was being equated with the boycott methods of the White Citizens Councils, I was forced for the first time to think seriously on the nature of the boycott. Up to this time I had uncritically accepted this method as our best course of action. Now certain doubts began to bother me. Were we following an ethical course of action? Is the boycott method basically unchristian? Isn't it a negative approach to the solution of a problem? Is it true that we would be following the course of some of the White Citizens Councils? Even if lasting practical results came from such a boycott, would immoral means justify moral ends? Each of these questions demanded honest answers.

I had to recognize that the boycott method could be used to unethical and unchristian ends. I had to concede, further, that this was the method used so often by the White Citizens Councils to deprive many Negroes, as well as white persons of good will, of the basic necessities of life. But certainly, I said to myself, our pending actions could not be interpreted in this light. Our purposes were altogether different. We would use this method to give birth to justice and freedom, and also to urge men to comply with the law of the land; the White Citizens Councils used it to perpetuate the reign of injustice and human servitude, and urged men to defy the law of the land. I reasoned, therefore, that the word "boycott" was really a misnomer for our proposed action. A boycott suggests an economic squeeze, leaving one bogged down in a negative. But we were concerned with the positive. Our concern would not be to put the bus company out of business, but to put justice in business.

As I thought further I came to see that what we were really doing was withdrawing our coöperation from an evil system, rather than merely withdrawing our economic support from the bus company. The bus company, being an external expression of the system, would naturally suffer, but the basic aim was to refuse to coöperate with evil. At this point I began to think about Thoreau's *Essay on Civil Disobedience*. I remembered how, as a college student, I had been moved when I first read this work. I became convinced that what we were preparing to do in Montgomery was related to what Thoreau had expressed. We were simply saying to the white community, "We can no longer lend our coöperation to an evil system."

Something began to say to me, "He who passively accepts evil is as much involved in it as he who helps to perpetrate it. He who accepts evil without protesting against it is really coöperating with it." When oppressed people willingly accept their oppression they only serve to give the oppressor a convenient justification for his acts. Often the oppressor goes along unaware of the evil involved in his oppression so long as the oppressed accepts it. So in order to be true to one's conscience and true to God, a righteous man has no alternative but to refuse to coöperate with an evil system. This I felt was the nature of our action. From this moment on I conceived of our movement as an act of massive noncoöperation. From then on I rarely used the word "boycott."

Wearied, but no longer doubtful about the morality of our proposed protest, I saw that the evening had arrived unnoticed. After several telephone calls I prepared to retire early. But soon after I was in bed our two-week-old daughter—Yolanda Denise—began crying; and shortly after that the telephone started ringing again. Clearly condemned to stay awake for some time longer, I used the time to think about other things. My wife and I discussed the possible success of the protest. Frankly, I still had doubts. Even though the word had gotten around amazingly well and the ministers had given the plan such crucial support, I still wondered whether the people had enough courage to follow through. I had seen so many admirable ventures fall through in Montgomery. Why should this be an exception? Coretta and I finally agreed that if we could get 60 per cent coöperation the protest would be a success.

Around midnight a call from one of the committee members informed me that every Negro taxi company in Montgomery had agreed to support the protest on Monday morning. Whatever our prospects of success, I was deeply encouraged by the untiring work that had been done by the ministers and civic leaders. This in itself was a unique accomplishment.

After the midnight call the phone stopped ringing. Just a few minutes earlier "Yoki" had stopped crying. Wearily, I said good night to Coretta, and with a strange mixture of hope and anxiety, I fell asleep.

IV

The Day of Days, December 5

My wife and I awoke earlier than usual on
Monday morning. We were up and fully dressed by five-thirty.
The day for the protest had arrived, and we were determined to
see the first act of this unfolding drama. I was still saying that if
we could get 60 per cent coöperation the venture would be a
success.

Fortunately, a bus stop was just five feet from our house. This
meant that we could observe the opening stages from our front
window. The first bus was to pass around six o'clock. And so
we waited through an interminable half hour. I was in the kitchen
drinking my coffee when I heard Coretta cry, "Martin, Martin,
come quickly!" I put down my cup and ran toward the living
room. As I approached the front window Coretta pointed joyfully
to a slowly moving bus: "Darling, it's empty!" I could hardly
believe what I saw. I knew that the South Jackson line, which
ran past our house, carried more Negro passengers than any other
line in Montgomery, and that this first bus was usually filled with
domestic workers going to their jobs. Would all of the other buses
follow the pattern that had been set by the first? Eagerly we
waited for the next bus. In fifteen minutes it rolled down the
street, and, like the first, it was empty. A third bus appeared,
and it too was empty of all but two white passengers.

I jumped in my car and for almost an hour I cruised down

every major street and examined every passing bus. During this hour, at the peak of the morning traffic, I saw no more than eight Negro passengers riding the buses. By this time I was jubilant. Instead of the 60 per cent coöperation we had hoped for, it was becoming apparent that we had reached almost 100 per cent. A miracle had taken place. The once dormant and quiescent Negro community was now fully awake.

All day long it continued. At the afternoon peak the buses were still as empty of Negro passengers as they had been in the morning. Students of Alabama State College, who usually kept the South Jackson bus crowded, were cheerfully walking or thumbing rides. Job holders had either found other means of transportation or made their way on foot. While some rode in cabs or private cars, others used less conventional means. Men were seen riding mules to work, and more than one horse-drawn buggy drove the streets of Montgomery that day.

During the rush hours the sidewalks were crowded with laborers and domestic workers, many of them well past middle age, trudging patiently to their jobs and home again, sometimes as much as twelve miles. They knew why they walked, and the knowledge was evident in the way they carried themselves. And as I watched them I knew that there is nothing more majestic than the determined courage of individuals willing to suffer and sacrifice for their freedom and dignity.

Many spectators had gathered at the bus stops to watch what was happening. At first they stood quietly, but as the day progressed they began to cheer the empty buses and laugh and make jokes. Noisy youngsters could be heard singing out, "No riders today." Trailing each bus through the Negro section were two policemen on motorcycles, assigned by the city commissioners, who claimed that Negro "goon squads" had been organized to keep other Negroes from riding the buses. In the course of the day the police succeeded in making one arrest. A college student who was helping an elderly woman across the street was charged with "intimidating passengers." But the "goon squads" existed only in the commission's imagination. No one was threatened or intimidated for riding the buses; the only harassment anyone faced was that of his own conscience.

Around nine-thirty in the morning I tore myself from the action of the city streets and headed for the crowded police court. Here Mrs. Parks was being tried for disobeying the city segregation ordinance. Her attorney, Fred D. Gray—the brilliant young Negro who later became the chief counsel for the protest movement— was on hand to defend her. After the judge heard the arguments, he found Mrs. Parks guilty and fined her ten dollars and court costs (a total of fourteen dollars). She appealed the case. This was one of the first clear-cut instances in which a Negro had been convicted for disobeying the segregation law. In the past, either cases like this had been dismissed or the people involved had been charged with disorderly conduct. So in a real sense the arrest and conviction of Mrs. Parks had a twofold impact: it was a precipitating factor to arouse the Negroes to positive action; and it was a test of the validity of the segregation law itself. I am sure that supporters of such prosecutions would have acted otherwise if they had had the prescience to look beyond the moment.

Leaving Mrs. Parks's trial, Ralph Abernathy, E. D. Nixon, and Rev. E. N. French—then minister of the Hilliard Chapel A. M. E. Zion Church—discussed the need for some organization to guide and direct the protest. Up to this time things had moved forward more or less spontaneously. These men were wise enough to see that the moment had now come for a clearer order and direction.

Meanwhile Roy Bennett had called several people together at

three o'clock to make plans for the evening mass meeting. Everyone present was elated by the tremendous success that had already attended the protest. But beneath this feeling was the question, where do we go from here? When E. D. Nixon reported on his discussion with Abernathy and French earlier in the day, and their suggestions for an *ad hoc* organization, the group responded enthusiastically. The next job was to elect the officers for the new organization.

As soon as Bennett had opened the nominations for president, Rufus Lewis spoke from the far corner of the room: "Mr. Chairman, I would like to nominate Reverend M. L. King for president." The motion was seconded and carried, and in a matter of minutes I was unanimously elected.

The action had caught me unawares. It had happened so quickly that I did not even have time to think it through. It is probable that if I had, I would have declined the nomination. Just three weeks before, several members of the local chapter of the NAACP had urged me to run for the presidency of that organization, assuring me that I was certain of election. After my wife and I had discussed the matter, we agreed that I should not then take on any heavy community responsibilities, since I had so recently finished my thesis, and needed to give more attention to my church work. But on this occasion events had moved too fast.

The election of the remaining officers was speedily completed: Rev. L. Roy Bennett, vice-president; Rev. U. J. Fields, recording secretary; Rev. E. N. French, corresponding secretary; Mrs. Erna A. Dungee, financial secretary; Mr. E. D. Nixon, treasurer. It was then agreed that all those present would constitute the executive board of the new organization. This board would serve as the coördinating agency of the whole movement. It was a well-balanced group, including ministers of all denominations, schoolteachers, businessmen, and two lawyers.

The new organization needed a name, and several were suggested. Someone proposed the Negro Citizens Committee; but this was rejected because it resembled too closely the White Citizens Council. Other suggestions were made and dismissed until finally Ralph Abernathy offered a name that was agreeable to all—the Montgomery Improvement Association (MIA).

With these organizational matters behind us, we turned to a discussion of the evening meeting. Several people, not wanting the reporters to know our future moves, suggested that we just sing and pray; if there were specific recommendations to be made to the people, these could be mimeographed and passed out secretly during the meeting. This, they felt, would leave the reporters in the dark. Others urged that something should be done to conceal the true identity of the leaders, feeling that if no particular name was revealed it would be safer for all involved. After a rather lengthy discussion, E. D. Nixon rose impatiently:

"We are acting like little boys," he said. "Somebody's name will have to be known, and if we are afraid we might just as well fold up right now. We must also be men enough to discuss our recommendations in the open; this idea of secretly passing something around on paper is a lot of bunk. The white folks are eventually going to find it out anyway. We'd better decide now if we are going to be fearless men or scared boys."

With this forthright statement the air was cleared. Nobody would again suggest that we try to conceal our identity or avoid facing the issue head on. Nixon's courageous affirmation had given new heart to those who were about to be crippled by fear.

It was unanimously agreed that the protest should continue until certain demands were met, and that a committee under the chairmanship of Ralph Abernathy would draw up these demands in the form of a resolution and present them to the evening mass meeting for approval. We worked out the remainder of the program quickly. Bennett would preside and I would make the main address. Remarks by a few other speakers, along with Scripture reading, prayer, hymns, and collection, would round out the program.

Immediately the resolution committee set to drafting its statement. Despite our satisfaction at the success of the protest so far, we were still concerned. Would the evening meeting be well attended? Could we hope that the fortitude and enthusiasm of the Negro community would survive more than one such day of hardship? Someone suggested that perhaps we should reconsider our decision to continue the protest. "Would it not be better," said the speaker, "to call off the protest while it is still a success rather than let it go on a few more days and fizzle out? We have already proved our united strength to the white community. If we stop now we can get anything we want from the bus company, simply because they will have the feeling that we can do it again. But if we continue, and most of the people return to the buses tomorrow or the next day, the white people will laugh at us, and we will end up getting nothing." This argument was so convincing that we almost resolved to end the protest. But we finally agreed to let the mass meeting—which was only about an hour off—be our guide. If the meeting was well attended and the people were enthusiastic, we would continue; otherwise we would call off the protest that night.

I went home for the first time since seven that morning, and found Coretta relaxing from a long day of telephone calls and general excitement. After we had brought each other up to date on the day's developments, I told her, somewhat hesitantly—

not knowing what her reaction would be—that I had been elected president of the new association. I need not have worried. Naturally surprised, she still saw that since the responsibility had fallen on me, I had no alternative but to accept it. She did not need to be told that we would now have even less time together, and she seemed undisturbed at the possible danger to all of us in my new position. "You know," she said quietly, "that whatever you do, you have my backing."

Reassured, I went to my study and closed the door. The minutes were passing fast. It was now six-thirty, and I had to leave no later than six-fifty to get to the meeting. This meant that I had only twenty minutes to prepare the most decisive speech of my life. As I thought of the limited time before me and the possible implications of this speech, I became possessed by fear. Each week I needed at least fifteen hours to prepare my Sunday sermon. Now I was faced with the inescapable task of preparing, in almost no time at all, a speech that was expected to give a sense of direction to a people imbued with a new and still unplumbed passion for justice. I was also conscious that reporters and television men would be there with their pencils and sound cameras poised to record my words and send them across the nation.

I was now almost overcome, obsessed by a feeling of inadequacy. In this state of anxiety, I had already wasted five minutes of the original twenty. With nothing left but faith in a power whose matchless strength stands over against the frailties and inadequacies of human nature, I turned to God in prayer. My words were brief and simple, asking God to restore my balance and to be with me in a time when I needed His guidance more than ever.

With less than fifteen minutes left, I began preparing an outline. In the midst of this, however, I faced a new and sobering dilemma: How could I make a speech that would be militant

enough to keep my people aroused to positive action and yet
moderate enough to keep this fervor within controllable and Christian bounds? I knew that many of the Negro people were victims
of bitterness that could easily rise to flood proportions. What
could I say to keep them courageous and prepared for positive
action and yet devoid of hate and resentment? Could the militant
and the moderate be combined in a single speech?

I decided that I had to face the challenge head on, and attempt
to combine two apparent irreconcilables. I would seek to arouse
the group to action by insisting that their self-respect was at stake
and that if they accepted such injustices without protesting, they
would betray their own sense of dignity and the eternal edicts of
God Himself. But I would balance this with a strong affirmation
of the Christian doctrine of love. By the time I had sketched an
outline of the speech in my mind, my time was up. Without stopping to eat supper (I had not eaten since morning) I said good-by
to Coretta and drove to the Holt Street Church.

Within five blocks of the church I noticed a traffic jam. Cars
were lined up as far as I could see on both sides of the street.
It was a moment before it occurred to me that all of these cars
were headed for the mass meeting. I had to park at least four
blocks from the church, and as I started walking I noticed that
hundreds of people were standing outside. In the dark night,
police cars circled slowly around the area, surveying the orderly,
patient, and good-humored crowd. The three or four thousand
people who could not get into the church were to stand cheerfully throughout the evening listening to the proceedings on the
loud-speakers that had been set up outside for their benefit. And
when, near the end of the meeting, these speakers were silenced
at the request of the white people in surrounding neighborhoods,

the crowd would still remain quietly, content simply to be present.

It took fully fifteen minutes to push my way through to the pastor's study, where Dr. Wilson told me that the church had been packed since five o'clock. By now my doubts concerning the continued success of our venture were dispelled. The question of calling off the protest was now academic. The enthusiasm of these thousands of people swept everything along like an onrushing tidal wave.

It was some time before the remaining speakers could push their way to the rostrum through the tightly packed church. When the meeting began it was almost half an hour late. The opening hymn was the old familiar "Onward Christian Soldiers," and when that mammoth audience stood to sing, the voices outside swelling the chorus in the church, there was a mighty ring like the glad echo of heaven itself.

Rev. W. F. Alford, minister of the Beulah Baptist Church, led the congregation in prayer, followed by a reading of the Scripture by Rev. U. J. Fields, minister of the Bell Street Baptist Church. Then the chairman introduced me. As the audience applauded, I rose and stood before the pulpit. Television cameras began to shoot from all sides. The crowd grew quiet.

Without manuscript or notes, I told the story of what had happened to Mrs. Parks. Then I reviewed the long history of abuses and insults that Negro citizens had experienced on the city buses. "But there comes a time," I said, "that people get tired. We are here this evening to say to those who have mistreated us so long that we are tired—tired of being segregated and humiliated; tired of being kicked about by the brutal feet of oppression." The congregation met this statement with fervent applause. "We had no alternative but to protest," I continued. "For many years, we have shown amazing patience. We have sometimes given our white brothers the feeling that we liked the way we were being treated. But we come here tonight to be saved from that patience that makes us patient with anything less than freedom and justice." Again the audience interrupted with applause.

Briefly I justified our actions, both morally and legally. "One of the great glories of democracy is the right to protest for right." Comparing our methods with those of the White Citizens Councils and the Ku Klux Klan, I pointed out that while "these organizations are protesting for the perpetuation of injustice in the community, we are protesting for the birth of justice in the community. Their methods lead to violence and lawlessness. But in our protest there will be no cross burnings. No white person will be taken from his home by a hooded Negro mob and brutally murdered. There will be no threats and intimidation. We will be guided by the highest principles of law and order."

With this groundwork for militant action, I moved on to words of caution. I urged the people not to force anybody to refrain from riding the buses. "Our method will be that of persuasion, not coercion. We will only say to the people, 'Let your conscience be your guide.' " Emphasizing the Christian doctrine of love, "our actions must be guided by the deepest principles of our Christian faith. Love must be our regulating ideal. Once again we must hear the words of Jesus echoing across the centuries: 'Love your enemies, bless them that curse you, and pray for them that despitefully use you.' If we fail to do this our protest will end up as a meaningless drama on the stage of history, and its memory will be shrouded with the ugly garments of shame. In spite of the mistreatment that we have confronted we must not become bitter, and end up by hating our white brothers. As Booker T. Washington said, 'Let no man pull you so low as to make you hate him.' " Once more the audience responded enthusiastically.

Then came my closing statement. "If you will protest courageously, and yet with dignity and Christian love, when the history
books are written in future generations, the historians will have
to pause and say, 'There lived a great people—a black people—
who injected new meaning and dignity into the veins of civilization.' This is our challenge and our overwhelming responsibilty."
As I took my seat the people rose to their feet and applauded.
I was thankful to God that the message had gotten over and that
the task of combining the militant and the moderate had been at
least partially accomplished. The people had been as enthusiastic
when I urged them to love as they were when I urged them to
protest.

As I sat listening to the continued applause I realized that this
speech had evoked more response than any speech or sermon I
had ever delivered, and yet it was virtually unprepared. I came
to see for the first time what the older preachers meant when they
said, "Open your mouth and God will speak for you." While I
would not let this experience tempt me to overlook the need for
continued preparation, it would always remind me that God can
transform man's weakness into his glorious opportunity.

When Mrs. Parks was introduced from the rostrum by E. N.
French, the audience responded by giving her a standing ovation.
She was their heroine. They saw in her courageous person the
symbol of their hopes and aspirations.

Now the time had come for the all-important resolution. Ralph
Abernathy read the words slowly and forcefully. The main substance of the resolution called upon the Negroes not to resume
riding the buses until (1) courteous treatment by the bus operators was guaranteed; (2) passengers were seated on a first-come,
first-served basis—Negroes seating from the back of the bus
toward the front while whites seated from the front toward the
back; (3) Negro bus operators were employed on predominantly

Negro routes. At the words "All in favor of the motion stand," every person to a man stood up, and those who were already standing raised their hands. Cheers began to ring out from both inside and outside. The motion was carried unanimously. The people had expressed their determination not to ride the buses until conditions were changed.

At this point I had to leave the meeting and rush to the other side of town to speak at a YMCA banquet. As I drove away my heart was full. I had never seen such enthusiasm for freedom. And yet this enthusiasm was tempered by amazing self-discipline. The unity of purpose and *esprit de corps* of these people had been indescribably moving. No historian would ever be able fully to describe this meeting and no sociologist would ever be able to interpret it adequately. One had to be a part of the experience really to understand it.

At the Ben Moore Hotel, as the elevator slowly moved up to the roof garden where the banquet was being held, I said to myself, the victory is already won, no matter how long we struggle to attain the three points of the resolution. It is a victory infinitely larger than the bus situation. The real victory was in the mass meeting, where thousands of black people stood revealed with a new sense of dignity and destiny.

Many will inevitably raise the question, why did this event take place in Montgomery, Alabama, in 1955? Some have suggested that the Supreme Court decision on school desegregation, handed down less than two years before, had given new hope of eventual justice to Negroes everywhere, and fired them with the necessary spark of encouragement to rise against their oppression. But although this might help to explain why the protest occurred when it did, it cannot explain why it happened in Montgomery.

Certainly, there is a partial explanation in the long history of

THE BEGINNING

Above: The fingerprinting of Mrs. Rosa Parks, whose refusal to move back in a bus and subsequent arrest touched off the Montgomery bus protest. *Left:* E. D. Nixon, veteran fighter for the cause of justice in Montgomery, who proposed the protest.

MASS

Week after week, crowds like the one above came together to sing and pray, to renew their courage, and to hear suggestions from their leaders. *Below,*

MEETINGS

three platform views: *left*, M. L. King, and a supporter; *center*, Ralph Abernathy; *right*, M. L. King, Robert Graetz, and Ralph Abernathy in prayer.

EFFECTIVE PROTEST

At a central pickup station, *above,* Montgomery's Negroes, young and old, wait to be driven home in the voluntary car pool. *Below:* a bus in operation during the protest.

injustice on the buses of Montgomery. The bus protest did not spring into being full grown as Athena sprang from the head of Zeus; it was the culmination of a slowly developing process. Mrs. Parks's arrest was the precipitating factor rather than the cause of the protest. The cause lay deep in the record of similar injustices. Almost everybody could point to an unfortunate episode that he himself had experienced or seen.

But there comes a time when people get tired of being trampled by oppression. There comes a time when people get tired of being plunged into the abyss of exploitation and nagging injustice. The story of Montgomery is the story of 50,000 such Negroes who were willing to substitute tired feet for tired souls, and walk the streets of Montgomery until the walls of segregation were finally battered by the forces of justice.

But neither is this the whole explanation. Negroes in other communities confronted conditions equally as bad, and often worse. So we cannot explain the Montgomery story merely in terms of the abuses that Negroes suffered there. Moreover, it cannot be explained by a preëxistent unity among the leaders, since we have seen that the Montgomery Negro community prior to the protest was marked by divided leadership, indifference, and complacency. Nor can it be explained by the appearance upon the scene of new leadership. The Montgomery story would have taken place if the leaders of the protest had never been born.

So every rational explanation breaks down at some point. There is something about the protest that is suprarational; it cannot be explained without a divine dimension. Some may call it a principle of concretion, with Alfred N. Whitehead; or a process of integration, with Henry N. Wieman; or Being-itself, with Paul Tillich; or a personal God. Whatever the name, some extra-human force labors to create a harmony out of the discords of the universe. There is a creative power that works to pull down mountains of evil and level hilltops of injustice. God still works through history His wonders to perform. It seems as though God had decided to use Montgomery as the proving ground for the struggle and triumph of freedom and justice in America. And what better place for it than the leading symbol of the Old South? It is one of the splendid ironies of our day that Montgomery, the Cradle of the Confederacy, is being transformed into Montgomery, the cradle of freedom and justice.

The day of days, Monday, December 5, 1955, was drawing to a close. We all prepared to go to our homes, not yet fully aware of what had happened. The deliberations of that brisk, cool night in December will not be forgotten. That night we were starting a movement that would gain national recognition; whose echoes would ring in the ears of people of every nation; a movement that would astound the oppressor, and bring new hope to the oppressed. That night was Montgomery's moment in history.

V

The Movement Gathers Momentum

AFTER ascending the mountain on Monday night, I woke up Tuesday morning urgently aware that I had to leave the heights and come back to earth. I was faced with a number of organizational decisions. The movement could no longer continue without careful planning.

I began to think of the various committees necessary to give the movement guidance and direction. First we needed a more permanent transportation committee, since the problem of getting the ex-bus riders about the city was paramount. I knew that we could not work out any system that would solve all the transportation problems of the nearly 17,500 Negroes who had formerly ridden the buses twice daily; even the most effective system that we could devise would still leave almost everyone walking a little more than he had done formerly. But a well-worked-out system could do a good deal to alleviate the problem.

We would also need to raise money to carry on the protest. Therefore, a finance committee was necessary. Since we would be having regular mass meetings, there must be a program committee for these occasions. And then, I reasoned, from time to time strategic decisions would have to be made; we needed the best minds of the association to think them through and then make recommendations to the executive board. So I felt that a strategy committee was essential.

With all of these things in mind I called a meeting of the executive board for Wednesday at ten o'clock in one of the larger rooms of the Alabama Negro Baptist Center. Every board member was present to applaud the report that after almost two and a half days the protest was still more than 99 per cent effective. There followed the appointment of the various committees. Because of the relatively small number on the executive board, it was necessary to place several people on more than one committee. As in all organizations, the problem of conflicting egos was involved, and the selections were guided by the desire to assure that the people on each committee could work well together. Rufus Lewis agreed to be chairman of the transportation committee, and Rev. R. J. Glasco, our host for the morning, chairman of the finance committee. The executive board was expanded to make it a broad cross section of the Negro community.*

The members of the strategy committee were appointed a few days later. This new committee brought together a dozen men and women who had already provided strong leadership in the early days of the protest, and whose clear thinking and courageous guidance were to be of inestimable help in the difficult decisions that still lay ahead. Besides the indispensable E. D. Nixon and our brilliant legal strategist, Fred Gray, the committee included Roy Bennett, who had chaired the first meeting to organize the protest and was to continue to give the movement his loyal support until he was transferred to a pastorate in California. H. H. Hubbard and A. W. Wilson, both Baptist ministers, represented the largest Negro congregations in Montgomery. Hubbard's stately presence brought a sense of security to every meeting that he attended; and his colleague, Wilson, who has held

* The members of the executive board and its committees are listed in the Appendix.

key positions in the Alabama Baptist State Convention, contributed his fine talent as an organizer and administrator.

Mrs. Euretta Adair, the wife of a prominent Montgomery physician, was a one-time faculty member of Tuskegee Institute who
combined a rich academic background with a passion for social
betterment. The current academic world was represented by Jo
Ann Robinson and J. E. Pierce, both faculty members of Alabama
State College, who had never allowed their secure positions to
make them indifferent to the problems of the people. Rufus Lewis,
a businessman who had also had a long interest in the Negroes'
struggle for first-class citizenship, was to display his conscientious-
ness and coöperative spirit as first chairman of the transportation
committee. When, after several months, the need for extending
the MIA's activities into such areas as voting became apparent,
he took the chairmanship of the new registration and voting
committee, a responsibility which he still holds.

W. J. Powell and S. S. Seay, like Bennett, were ministers of the
A.M.E. Zion Church. Powell brought a cool head and an even
temper to the problems that confronted the strategy committee
in these tempestuous days. S. S. Seay's was one of the few clerical
voices that, in the years preceding the protest, had lashed out
against the injustices heaped on the Negro, and urged his people
to a greater appreciation of their own worth. A dynamic preacher,
his addresses from time to time at the weekly mass meetings raised
the spirits of all who heard him.

The final member of the strategy committee was already in the
forefront of the forces of protest. Ralph Abernathy was another
of the few Negro clergymen who had long been active in civic
affairs. Although he was then only twenty-nine, his devotion to
the cause of freedom was already beyond question. With his short,
stocky frame and his thoughtful expression, he looked older than
his years. But a boyish smile always lurked beneath the surface of

his face. Ralph's slow movements and slow, easy talk were decep-
tive. For he was an indefatigable worker and a sound thinker,
possessed of a fertile mind. As a speaker, he was persuasive and
dynamic, with the gift of laughing people into positive action.
When things became languid around the mass meetings, Ralph
Abernathy infused his audiences with new life and ardor. The
people loved and respected him as a symbol of courage and
strength.

From the beginning of the protest Ralph Abernathy was my
closest associate and most trusted friend. We prayed together and
made important decisions together. His ready good humor light-
ened many tense moments. Whenever I went out of town I always
left him in charge of the important business of the association,
knowing that it was in safe hands. After Bennett left Montgomery,
Ralph became first vice-president of the MIA, and has held that
position ever since with dignity and efficiency.

These were the people with whom, from the beginning, I
worked most closely. As time went on others were added. Among
these, an early recruit to the executive committee was Rev.
Robert Graetz, whom I had first met in the Council on Human
Relations. This boyish-looking white minister of the Negro Trinity
Lutheran Church was a constant reminder to us in the trying
months of the protest that many white people as well as Negroes
were applying the "love-thy-neighbor-as-thyself" teachings of
Christianity in their daily lives. Other close associates who were
later added to the board were Clarence W. Lee, a tall distinguished-looking mortician, whose sound business ability became
a great asset to the organization, and Moses W. Jones, a prominent
physician, who later became the second vice-president of the
MIA.

We met at all hours, whenever a new emergency demanded
attention. It was not unusual to find some of us talking things

over in one of our homes at two-thirty in the morning. While our wives plied us with coffee, and joined the informal discussion, we laid plans and arrived at agreements on policy. No parliamentary rules were necessary in this small group; the rule of the majority was tacitly accepted.

In the early stages of the protest the problem of transportation demanded most of our attention. The labor and ingenuity that went into that task is one of the most interesting sides of the Montgomery story. For the first few days we had depended on the Negro taxi companies who had agreed to transport the people for the same ten-cent fare that they paid on the buses. Except for a few private cars that had been volunteered, these taxis had provided the only transportation. But during the first "negotiation meeting" that we were to hold with the city commission on Thursday, December 8, Police Commissioner Sellers mentioned in passing that there was a law that limited the taxis to a minimum fare. I caught this hint and realized that Commissioner Sellers would probably use this point to stop the taxis from assisting in the protest.

At that moment I remembered that some time previously my good friend Rev. Theodore Jemison had lead a bus boycott in Baton Rouge, Louisiana. Knowing that Jemison and his associates had set up an effective private car pool, I put in a long-distance call to ask him for suggestions for a similar pool in Montgomery. As I expected, his painstaking description of the Baton Rouge experience was invaluable. I passed on word of Sellers' remark and Jemison's advice to the transportation committee and suggested that we immediately begin setting up a pool in order to offset the confusion which could come if the taxis were eliminated from service.

Fortunately, a mass meeting was being held that night. There I asked all those who were willing to offer their cars to give us their names, addresses, telephone numbers, and the hours that they could drive, before leaving the meeting. The response was tremendous. More than a hundred and fifty signed slips volunteering their automobiles. Some who were not working offered to drive in the car pool all day; others volunteered a few hours before and after work. Practically all of the ministers offered to drive whenever they were needed.

On Friday afternoon, as I had predicted, the police commissioner issued an order to all of the cab companies reminding them that by law they had to charge a minimum fare of forty-five cents, and saying that failure to comply would be a legal offense. This brought an end to the cheap taxi service.

Our answer was to call hastily on our volunteers, who responded immediately. They started out simply by cruising the streets of Montgomery with no particular system. On Saturday the ministers agreed to go to their pulpits the following day and seek additional recruits. Again the response was tremendous. With the new additions, the number of cars swelled to about three hundred.

The real job was just beginning—that of working out some system for these three hundred-odd automobiles, to replace their haphazard movement around the city. During the days that followed, the transportation committee worked every evening into the morning hours attempting to set up an adequate system. Several of Jemison's suggestions proved profitable. Finally, the decision was made to set up "dispatch" and "pick-up" stations, points at which passengers would assemble for transportation to their jobs and home again. The dispatch stations would be open from 6:00 to 10:00 A.M., and the pick-up stations from 3:00 to 7:00 P.M.

Next came the difficult task of selecting sites for the stations that would adequately cover the whole city. While most of us found it relatively easy to think of dispatch stations, since they would be in Negro sections of town, we discovered that we were at a loss in selecting pick-up stations. The problem was that the vast majority of those who had ridden the buses worked for white employers, and the pick-up stations would therefore have to be in white sections, of which we had little, if any, knowledge. Fortunately, however, we had two postal workers on the committee, who knew the city from end to end. With their assistance and the aid of a city map we began working with new facility.

At this time, R. J. Glasco was prominent on the transportation committee along with the chairman, Rufus Lewis. These men, with the assistance of the whole committee, worked assiduously to lay out the plan. By Tuesday, December 13, the system had been worked out. Thousands of mimeographed leaflets were distributed throughout the Negro community with a list of the forty-eight dispatch and the forty-two pick-up stations. Most of the dispatch stations were located at the Negro churches. These churches coöperated by opening their doors early each morning so that the waiting passengers could be seated, and many of them provided heat on cold mornings. Each of the private cars was assigned to one of the dispatch and one of the pick-up stations, the number of cars assigned to each station determined by the number of persons using it. By far the most heavily used station was a Negro-owned parking lot located in the downtown section of Montgomery. It was a combination pick-up and dispatch point.

In a few days this system was working astonishingly well. The white opposition was so impressed at this miracle of quick organization that they had to admit in a White Citizens Council meeting that the pool moved with "military precision." The MIA had worked out in a few nights a transportation problem that the bus company had grappled with for many years.

Despite this success, so profoundly had the spirit of the protest become a part of the people's lives that sometimes they even preferred to walk when a ride was available. The act of walking, for

many, had become of symbolic importance. Once a pool driver
stopped beside an elderly woman who was trudging along with
obvious difficulty.

"Jump in, grandmother," he said. "You don't need to walk."

She waved him on. "I'm not walking for myself," she explained.
"I'm walking for my children and my grandchildren." And she
continued toward home on foot.

While the largest number of drivers were ministers, their ranks
were augmented by housewives, teachers, businessmen, and unskilled laborers. At least three white men from the air bases drove
in the pool during their off-duty hours. One of the most faithful
drivers was Mrs. A. W. West, who had early shown her enthusiasm
for the protest idea by helping to call the civic leaders to the
first organizing meeting. Every morning she drove her large green
Cadillac to her assigned dispatch station, and for several hours
in the morning and again in the afternoon one could see this distinguished and handsome gray-haired chauffeur driving people
to work and home again.

Another loyal driver was Jo Ann Robinson. Attractive, fair-
skinned, and still youthful, Jo Ann came by her goodness naturally.
She did not need to learn her nonviolence from any book. Apparently indefatigable, she, perhaps more than any other person,
was active on every level of the protest. She took part in both
the executive board and the strategy committee meetings. When
the MIA newsletter was inaugurated a few months after the
protest began, she became its editor. She was sure to be present
whenever negotiations were in progress. And although she carried a full teaching load at Alabama State, she still found time to
drive both morning and afternoon.

The ranks of our drivers were further swelled from an unfore-
seen source. Many white housewives, whatever their commitment
to segregation, had no intention of being without their maids.

And so every day they drove to the Negro sections to pick up their servants and returned them at night. Certainly, if selfishness was a part of the motive, in many cases affection for a faithful servant also played its part. There was some humor in the tacit understandings—and sometimes mutually accepted misunderstandings—between these white employers and their Negro servants. One old domestic, an influential matriarch to many young relatives in Montgomery, was asked by her wealthy employer, "Isn't this bus boycott terrible?"

The old lady responded: "Yes, ma'am, it sure is. And I just told all my young'uns that this kind of thing is white folks' business and we just stay off the buses till they get this whole thing settled."

As time moved on the pool continued to grow and expand. Rev. B. J. Simms, college professor and pastor of a Baptist church in Tuskegee, took over the chairmanship of the committee, adding his own creative ideas to the good work of his predecessor, Rufus Lewis. Soon the transportation office had grown to a staff of six. More than twenty-five people were employed as all-day drivers, working six days a week. In most of the stations, dispatchers were employed to keep things running smoothly and divide the passengers on the basis of the direction in which they were going. A chief dispatcher—Rev. J. H. Cherry—stationed at the downtown parking lot proved to be of inestimable value. Richard Harris, a Negro pharmacist, was also a great asset to the transportation system. From the office of his drugstore he dispatched cars by telephone from early morning till late evening. Visitors were always astonished to see this young energetic businessman standing with a telephone at his ear dispatching cars and filling a prescription simultaneously.

Finally, a fleet of more than fifteen new station wagons was added. Each of these 1956 cars was registered as the property of a different church, and the name of the sponsoring church was emblazoned on the front and side of each vehicle. As these "rolling churches" carried their spirited loads of passengers along to work, an occasional sound of hymn-singing came from their windows. Pedestrians who could find no room in the crowded vehicles waved as their own "church" passed by, and walked on with new heart.

Altogether the operation of the motor pool represented organization and coördination at their best. Reporters and visitors from all over the country looked upon the system as a unique accomplishment. But the job took money. For a while the MIA had been able to carry on through local contributions. Week after week, wealthy or poor, the Negroes of Montgomery gave what they could, even though sometimes there was only a dime or a quarter to put into the collection box. But as the pool grew and other expenses mounted, it was evident that we needed additional funds to carry on. The cost of running the MIA had increased to $5000 a month.

Fortunately the liberal coverage of the press had carried the word of our struggle across the world. Although we never made a public appeal for funds, contributions began to pour in from as far away as Tokyo. MIA leaders were invited to cities all over the country to appear in fund-raising meetings. Every day brought visitors bearing gifts, and every mail brought checks. Sometimes the gift was as large as $5000, sometimes only a single dollar bill, but altogether they added up to nearly $250,000.

The largest response came from church groups—particularly, though by no means only, Negro churches. Several ministerial associations contributed generously. It would be safe to say that churches in almost every city in the United States sent help. Labor, civic, and social groups were our stanch supporters, and in many communities new organizations were founded just to support the protest. Almost every branch of the NAACP responded generously to a letter from Roy Wilkins, the executive secretary, urging them to give moral and financial support to the movement; and this was only one of the many ways in which the NAACP was to lend its strength in the days ahead.

Contributions came from many individuals, too, both white and Negro, here and abroad. Often these were accompanied by letters that raised our spirits and helped to break the sense of isolation that surrounded us in our own community. From Pennsylvania came a check for a hundred dollars, along with a note in the spidery handwriting of an elderly gentlewoman: "Your work . . . is outstanding and unprecedented in the history of our country. Indeed, it is epoch-making and it should have a far-reaching effect. . . . 'Not by might, nor by power, but by my spirit, saith the Lord'—this might well be the motto of the Montgomery Improvement Association." A former federal judge wrote: "You have shown that decency and courage will eventually prevail. . . . The immediate issue has not been won as yet but such faith and determination is bound to be triumphant and the persecutors must themselves by this time come to realize that they are fighting a cruel but losing effort. The entire nation salutes you and prays for your early relief and victory."

From Singapore came the assurance that "what you are doing is a real inspiration to us here in the part of the world where the struggle between democracy and communism is raging." The crew of a ship at sea cabled: "We offer a prayer in sympathy in the fight for justice." And a Swiss woman whose "friends and husband do not understand" saved her own money to send us one of our largest individual contributions. "Since I have no possibility," she wrote, "to help you in an efficacious manner (this is such a bad feeling, believe me) and I burningly would like to do just something, I send you these 500 dollars. . . . You would make me a very great pleasure, if you accepted, because what else could I do?"

Truly the Montgomery movement had spoken to a responsive world. But while these letters brought us much-needed encouragement, they were also the source of persistent frustration for me. The MIA lacked proper office facilities and staff, and due to the shortage of secretarial help most of the early letters had to go unanswered. Even financial contributions were often unacknowledged. The more I thought of my inability to cope with these matters, the more disturbed I became.

My frustration was augmented by the fact that for several weeks after the protest began, people were calling me at every hour of the day and night. The phone would start ringing as early as five o'clock in the morning and seldom stopped before midnight. Sometimes it was an ex-bus rider asking me to arrange to get her to work and back home at a certain hour. Sometimes it was a driver complaining about uncoöperative passengers or a passenger complaining about a temperamental driver. Sometimes a driver's car had broken down. Sometimes it was a maid who had been threatened with firing by her employer if she continued to stay off the buses, and sometimes a person who simply wanted to know where the nearest pick-up station was located. From time to time someone called to say that a certain driver was charging his passengers, and needed to be stopped before his acts jeopardized the legal status of the whole system.

We came to see the necessity of having a well-staffed office to face such problems as these. At first we attempted to run it with volunteer secretarial help. But this was not sufficient. So we hired a full-time secretary to do the regular work of the association, and set up a transportation office with a secretary to work

directly in that area. As time went on the correspondence became so heavy and the transportation work so detailed that it
was necessary to employ an office staff of ten persons. With the
growth of the office staff and other administrative matters, the
board finally supplied me with an executive assistant, Rev. R. J.
Glasco. All of these steps—the hiring of office secretaries, setting
up a transportation office, and the hiring of an executive assistant
—served to lighten an almost unbearable load, and helped me to
regain my bearings.

But the job of getting the movement going was not yet finished.
There was still the task of finding permanent office space to house
the MIA. This problem proved to be unexpectedly difficult, and
we were forced to move no less than four times before we found
a relatively permanent location.

The first office was in the Alabama Negro Baptist Center. Here
we had access to two large rooms and also an assembly room for
board meetings. Both location and facilities met our needs. As
soon as we were settled there, however, the white officials of the
Montgomery Baptist Association—the organization which supplied the largest amount of money for the operation of the center
—called the trustees of the center into a conference and suggested
that "for the good of the center" and "the good of the community"
the MIA headquarters should be moved. Although it was never
explicitly stated, we could discern an implicit threat to withdraw
financial assistance if the request were not complied with immediately.

Seeing that we were almost out of doors, Rufus Lewis offered
the MIA the use of his club—the Citizens Club. He set at our
disposal a large room, which was usually used for banquets, and
a small room for the transportation committee. But after we had
been in the Citizens Club for a few weeks Mr. Lewis got word
from reliable sources that if the MIA remained there his license

would be revoked on the grounds that the club was being used
as an office building. In this emergency the First Baptist Church
offered its limited office space as a temporary abode.

Finally, we discovered that the new building of the Bricklayers
Union had available space which would serve our purposes well.
Here the white community could not force us out, since most of
the members and all of the officers of the union that owned the
building were Negroes. With this consideration in mind we
decided to rent space there.

By then the office staff was exhausted. They had moved back
and forth all over the city. In this continuous moving process some
important letters had almost certainly been lost and significant
records misplaced. But at least we now had an office with an air
of permanence. For the first time we had enough space to work
with a modicum of peace and security.

The biggest job in getting any movement off the ground is to
keep together the people who form it. This task requires more
than a common aim: it demands a philosophy that wins and holds
the people's allegiance; and it depends upon open channels of
communication between the people and their leaders. All of these
elements were present in Montgomery.

From the beginning a basic philosophy guided the movement.
This guiding principle has since been referred to variously as
nonviolent resistance, noncoöperation, and passive resistance. But
in the first days of the protest none of these expressions was
mentioned; the phrase most often heard was "Christian love." It
was the Sermon on the Mount, rather than a doctrine of passive
resistance, that initially inspired the Negroes of Montgomery to
dignified social action. It was Jesus of Nazareth that stirred the
Negroes to protest with the creative weapon of love.

As the days unfolded, however, the inspiration of Mahatma

Gandhi began to exert its influence. I had come to see early that the Christian doctrine of love operating through the Gandhian method of nonviolence was one of the most potent weapons available to the Negro in his struggle for freedom. About a week after the protest started, a white woman who understood and sympathized with the Negroes' efforts wrote a letter to the editor of the *Montgomery Advertiser* comparing the bus protest with the Gandhian movement in India. Miss Juliette Morgan, sensitive and frail, did not long survive the rejection and condemnation of the white community, but long before she died in the summer of 1957 the name of Mahatma Gandhi was well-known in Montgomery. People who had never heard of the little brown saint of India were now saying his name with an air of familiarity. Nonviolent resistance had emerged as the technique of the movement, while love stood as the regulating ideal. In other words, Christ furnished the spirit and motivation, while Gandhi furnished the method.

This philosophy was disseminated mainly through the regular mass meetings which were held in the various Negro churches of the city. For the first several months the meetings occurred twice a week—on Mondays and Thursdays—but in the fall of 1956 the number was reduced to one a week, a schedule that continues to this day. At the beginning of the protest these twice-a-week get-togethers were indispensable channels of communication, since Montgomery had neither a Negro-owned radio station nor a widely read Negro newspaper.

The meetings rotated from church to church. The speakers represented the various denominations, thus removing any grounds for sectarian jealousy. One of the glories of the Montgomery movement was that Baptists, Methodists, Lutherans, Presbyterians, Episcopalians, and others all came together with a willingness to transcend denominational lines. Although no

Catholic priests were actively involved in the protest, many of
their parishioners took part. All joined hands in the bond of
Christian love. Thus the mass meetings accomplished on Monday
and Thursday nights what the Christian Church had failed to
accomplish on Sunday mornings.

The mass meetings also cut across class lines. The vast majority
present were working people; yet there was always an appreciable
number of professionals in the audience. Physicians, teachers, and
lawyers sat or stood beside domestic workers and unskilled
laborers. The Ph.D's and the no "D's" were bound together in
a common venture. The so-called "big Negroes" who owned cars
and had never ridden the buses came to know the maids and the
laborers who rode the buses every day. Men and women who had
been separated from each other by false standards of class were
now singing and praying together in a common struggle for freedom and human dignity.

The meetings started at seven, but people came hours ahead
of time to get a seat. It was not uncommon to find the churches
completely filled by five in the afternoon. Some read papers and
books while they waited; others joined in group singing. Usually
the hymns preceding the meeting were unaccompanied lined
tunes of low pitch and long meter. One could not help but be
moved by these traditional songs, which brought to mind the
long history of the Negro's suffering.

By the time the meeting started, virtually every space was taken,
and hundreds often overflowed into the streets. Many late-comers
learned to bring their own folding stools, and many others stayed
away because they knew that it would be impossible to find a
space. At first we tried to deal with this problem by having as
many as five simultaneous meetings in different parts of the city,
each with the same theme and pattern. For several weeks I made
it a practice to appear at all five meetings, but this was a strenu-

ous undertaking. Moreover, the people began to insist that they wanted to be together; so we soon went back to the one big meeting.

The evenings followed a simple pattern: songs, prayer, Scripture reading, opening remarks by the president, collection, reports from various committees, and a "pep talk." The latter was the main address of the evening, usually given by a different minister at each meeting. The "pep talk" acquired its rather undignified title during the early days of the protest, when the primary purpose was to give the people new "pep" and enthusiasm for the struggle ahead. Night after night the group was admonished to love rather than hate, and urged to be prepared to suffer violence if necessary but never to inflict it. Every "pep" speaker was asked to make nonviolence a central part of his theme.

Inevitably, a speaker would occasionally get out of hand. One minister, after lashing out against the whites in distinctly untheological terms, ended by referring to the extremists of the white community as "dirty crackers." After the meeting he was politely but firmly informed that his insulting phrases were out of place. But such instances of offensive language were surprisingly few.

In my weekly remarks as president, I stressed that the use of violence in our struggle would be both impractical and immoral. To meet hate with retaliatory hate would do nothing but intensify the existence of evil in the universe. Hate begets hate; violence begets violence; toughness begets a greater toughness. We must meet the forces of hate with the power of love; we must meet physical force with soul force. Our aim must never be to defeat or humiliate the white man, but to win his friendship and understanding.

From the beginning the people responded to this philosophy with amazing ardor. To be sure, there were some who were slow to concur. Occasionally members of the executive board would say to me in private that we needed a more militant approach. They looked upon nonviolence as weak and compromising. Others felt that at least a modicum of violence would convince the white people that the Negroes meant business and were not afraid. A member of my church came to me one day and solemnly suggested that it would be to our advantage to "kill off" eight or ten white people. "This is the only language these white folks will understand," he said. "If we fail to do this they will think we're afraid. We must show them we're not afraid any longer." Besides, he thought, if a few white persons were killed the federal government would inevitably intervene and this, he was certain, would benefit us.

Still others felt that they could be nonviolent only if they were not attacked personally. They would say: "If nobody bothers me, I will bother nobody. If nobody hits me, I will hit nobody. But if I am hit, I will hit back." They thus drew a moral line between aggressive and retaliatory violence. But in spite of these honest disagreements, the vast majority were willing to try the experiment.

The very spirit of the meetings revealed their nature. The songs, the prayers, the Scripture readings, and the speeches were by and large nonviolent in tone. A favorite Scriptural passage was, "And now abideth faith, hope, love, these three; but the greatest of these is love." Another was the famous dialogue on forgiveness between Jesus and Peter: "Then came Peter to him, and said, Lord, how oft shall my brother sin against me, and I forgive him? till seven times? Jesus saith unto him, I say not unto thee, Until seven times: but, Until seventy times seven." For the mass-meeting audiences, these Scriptural admonitions were not abstractions that came to them from a distance across the centuries; they had a personal and immediate meaning for them today.

Throughout, there was a surprising lack of bitterness, even when speakers referred to the latest white insult or act of terrorism. And when, later on, the MIA was to be faced with its only serious internal crisis, the people showed that they could handle dissension among themselves with equal restraint, refraining not only from physical violence but also from violence of spirit.

In a real sense, Montgomery's Negroes showed themselves willing to grapple with a new approach to the crisis in race relations. It is probably true that most of them did not believe in nonviolence as a philosophy of life, but because of their confidence in their leaders and because nonviolence was presented to them as a simple expression of Christianity in action, they were willing to use it as a technique. Admittedly, nonviolence in the truest sense is not a strategy that one uses simply because it is expedient at the moment; nonviolence is ultimately a way of life that men live by because of the sheer morality of its claim. But even granting this, the willingness to use nonviolence as a technique is a step forward. For he who goes this far is more likely to adopt nonviolence later as a way of life.

VI

Pilgrimage to Nonviolence

Often the question has arisen concerning my own intellectual pilgrimage to nonviolence. In order to get at this question it is necessary to go back to my early teens in Atlanta. I had grown up abhorring not only segregation but also the oppressive and barbarous acts that grew out of it. I had passed spots where Negroes had been savagely lynched, and had watched the Ku Klux Klan on its rides at night. I had seen police brutality with my own eyes, and watched Negroes receive the most tragic injustice in the courts. All of these things had done something to my growing personality. I had come perilously close to resenting all white people.

I had also learned that the inseparable twin of racial injustice was economic injustice. Although I came from a home of economic security and relative comfort, I could never get out of my mind the economic insecurity of many of my playmates and the tragic poverty of those living around me. During my late teens I worked two summers, against my father's wishes—he never wanted my brother and me to work around white people because of the oppressive conditions—in a plant that hired both Negroes and whites. Here I saw economic injustice firsthand, and realized that the poor white was exploited just as much as the Negro. Through these early experiences I grew up deeply conscious of the varieties of injustice in our society.

So when I went to Atlanta's Morehouse College as a freshman in 1944 my concern for racial and economic justice was already substantial. During my student days at Morehouse I read Thoreau's *Essay on Civil Disobedience* for the first time. Fascinated by the idea of refusing to coöperate with an evil system, I was so deeply moved that I reread the work several times. This was my first intellectual contact with the theory of nonviolent resistance.

Not until I entered Crozer Theological Seminary in 1948, however, did I begin a serious intellectual quest for a method to eliminate social evil. Although my major interest was in the fields of theology and philosophy, I spent a great deal of time reading the works of the great social philosophers. I came early to Walter Rauschenbusch's *Christianity and the Social Crisis,* which left an indelible imprint on my thinking by giving me a theological basis for the social concern which had already grown up in me as a result of my early experiences. Of course there were points at which I differed with Rauschenbusch. I felt that he had fallen victim to the nineteenth-century "cult of inevitable progress" which led him to a superficial optimism concerning man's nature. Moreover, he came perilously close to identifying the Kingdom of God with a particular social and economic system—a tendency which should never befall the Church. But in spite of these shortcomings Rauschenbusch had done a great service for the Christian Church by insisting that the gospel deals with the whole man, not only his soul but his body; not only his spiritual well-being but his material well-being. It has been my conviction ever since reading Rauschenbusch that any religion which professes to be concerned about the souls of men and is not concerned about the social and economic conditions that scar the soul, is a spiritually moribund religion only waiting for the day to be buried. It well has been said: "A religion that ends with the individual, ends."

After reading Rauschenbusch, I turned to a serious study of the social and ethical theories of the great philosophers, from Plato and Aristotle down to Rousseau, Hobbes, Bentham, Mill, and Locke. All of these masters stimulated my thinking—such as it was—and, while finding things to question in each of them, I nevertheless learned a great deal from their study.

During the Christmas holidays of 1949 I decided to spend my spare time reading Karl Marx to try to understand the appeal of communism for many people. For the first time I carefully scrutinized *Das Kapital* and *The Communist Manifesto*. I also read some interpretive works on the thinking of Marx and Lenin. In reading such Communist writings I drew certain conclusions that have remained with me as convictions to this day. First I rejected their materialistic interpretation of history. Communism, avowedly secularistic and materialistic, has no place for God. This I could never accept, for as a Christian I believe that there is a creative personal power in this universe who is the ground and essence of all reality—a power that cannot be explained in materialistic terms. History is ultimately guided by spirit, not matter. Second, I strongly disagreed with communism's ethical relativism. Since for the Communist there is no divine government, no absolute moral order, there are no fixed, immutable principles; consequently almost anything—force, violence, murder, lying— is a justifiable means to the "millennial" end. This type of relativism was abhorrent to me. Constructive ends can never give absolute moral justification to destructive means, because in the final analysis the end is preëxistent in the mean. Third, I opposed communism's political totalitarianism. In communism the individual ends up in subjection to the state. True, the Marxist would argue that the state is an "interim" reality which is to be eliminated when the classless society emerges; but the state is the end while it lasts, and man only a means to that end. And if any man's so-called rights or liberties stand in the way of that end, they are simply swept aside. His liberties of expression, his freedom to vote, his freedom to listen to what news he likes or to choose his books are all restricted. Man becomes hardly more, in communism, than a depersonalized cog in the turning wheel of the state.

This deprecation of individual freedom was objectionable to me. I am convinced now, as I was then, that man is an end because he is a child of God. Man is not made for the state; the state is made for man. To deprive man of freedom is to relegate him to the status of a thing, rather than elevate him to the status of a person. Man must never be treated as a means to the end of the state, but always as an end within himself.

Yet, in spite of the fact that my response to communism was and is negative, and I considered it basically evil, there were points at which I found it challenging. The late Archbishop of Canterbury, William Temple, referred to communism as a Christian heresy. By this he meant that communism had laid hold of certain truths which are essential parts of the Christian view of things, but that it had bound up with them concepts and practices which no Christian could ever accept or profess. Communism challenged the late Archbishop and it should challenge every Christian—as it challenged me—to a growing concern about social justice. With all of its false assumptions and evil methods, communism grew as a protest against the hardships of the underprivileged. Communism in theory emphasized a classless society, and a concern for social justice, though the world knows from sad experience that in practice it created new classes and a new lexicon of injustice. The Christian ought always to be challenged by any protest against unfair treatment of the poor, for Christianity is itself such a protest, nowhere expressed more eloquently than in Jesus' words: "The Spirit of the Lord is upon me, because

he hath anointed me to preach the gospel to the poor; he hath
sent me to heal the brokenhearted, to preach deliverance to the
captives, and recovering of sight to the blind, to set at liberty
them that are bruised, to preach the acceptable year of the Lord."

I also sought systematic answers to Marx's critique of modern
bourgeois culture. He presented capitalism as essentially a struggle between the owners of the productive resources and the
workers, whom Marx regarded as the real producers. Marx interpreted economic forces as the dialectical process by which society
moved from feudalism through capitalism to socialism, with the
primary mechanism of this historical movement being the struggle
between economic classes whose interests were irreconcilable.
Obviously this theory left out of account the numerous and significant complexities—political, economic, moral, religious, and
psychological—which played a vital role in shaping the constel-
lation of institutions and ideas known today as Western civilization. Moreover, it was dated in the sense that the capitalism Marx
wrote about bore only a partial resemblance to the capitalism we
know in this country today.

But in spite of the shortcomings of his analysis, Marx had
raised some basic questions. I was deeply concerned from my
early teen days about the gulf between superfluous wealth and
abject poverty, and my reading of Marx made me ever more
conscious of this gulf. Although modern American capitalism
had greatly reduced the gap through social reforms, there was
still need for a better distribution of wealth. Moreover, Marx had
revealed the danger of the profit motive as the sole basis of an
economic system: capitalism is always in danger of inspiring men
to be more concerned about making a living than making a life.
We are prone to judge success by the index of our salaries or the
size of our automobiles, rather than by the quality of our service
and relationship to humanity—thus capitalism can lead to a

practical materialism that is as pernicious as the materialism taught by communism.

In short, I read Marx as I read all of the influential historical thinkers—from a dialectical point of view, combining a partial yes and a partial no. In so far as Marx posited a metaphysical materialism, an ethical relativism, and a strangulating totalitarianism, I responded with an unambiguous "no"; but in so far as he pointed to weaknesses of traditional capitalism, contributed to the growth of a definite self-consciousness in the masses, and challenged the social conscience of the Christian churches, I responded with a definite "yes."

My reading of Marx also convinced me that truth is found neither in Marxism nor in traditional capitalism. Each represents a partial truth. Historically capitalism failed to see the truth in collective enterprise and Marxism failed to see the truth in individual enterprise. Nineteenth-century capitalism failed to see that life is social and Marxism failed and still fails to see that life is individual and personal. The Kingdom of God is neither the thesis of individual enterprise nor the antithesis of collective enterprise, but a synthesis which reconciles the truths of both.

During my stay at Crozer, I was also exposed for the first time to the pacifist position in a lecture by Dr. A. J. Muste. I was deeply moved by Dr. Muste's talk, but far from convinced of the practicability of his position. Like most of the students of Crozer, I felt that while war could never be a positive or absolute good, it could serve as a negative good in the sense of preventing the spread and growth of an evil force. War, horrible as it is, might be preferable to surrender to a totalitarian system—Nazi, Fascist, or Communist.

During this period I had about despaired of the power of love in solving social problems. Perhaps my faith in love was tem-

porarily shaken by the philosophy of Nietzsche. I had been reading parts of *The Genealogy of Morals* and the whole of *The Will
to Power*. Nietzsche's glorification of power—in his theory all life
expressed the will to power—was an outgrowth of his contempt
for ordinary morals. He attacked the whole of the Hebraic-Chris-
tian morality—with its virtues of piety and humility, its other-
worldliness and its attitude toward suffering—as the glorification
of weakness, as making virtues out of necessity and impotence.
He looked to the development of a superman who would surpass
man as man surpassed the ape.

Then one Sunday afternoon I traveled to Philadelphia to hear
a sermon by Dr. Mordecai Johnson, president of Howard University. He was there to preach for the Fellowship House of Philadelphia. Dr. Johnson had just returned from a trip to India, and,
to my great interest, he spoke of the life and teachings of
Mahatma Gandhi. His message was so profound and electrifying
that I left the meeting and bought a half-dozen books on Gandhi's
life and works.

Like most people, I had heard of Gandhi, but I had never
studied him seriously. As I read I became deeply fascinated by
his campaigns of nonviolent resistance. I was particularly moved
by the Salt March to the Sea and his numerous fasts. The whole
concept of "Satyagraha" (*Satya* is truth which equals love, and
agraha is force; "Satyagraha," therefore, means truth-force or love
force) was profoundly significant to me. As I delved deeper into
the philosophy of Gandhi my skepticism concerning the power
of love gradually diminished, and I came to see for the first time
its potency in the area of social reform. Prior to reading Gandhi,
I had about concluded that the ethics of Jesus were only effective
in individual relationship. The "turn the other cheek" philosophy
and the "love your enemies" philosophy were only valid, I felt,

when individuals were in conflict with other individuals; when racial groups and nations were in conflict a more realistic approach seemed necessary. But after reading Gandhi, I saw how utterly mistaken I was.

Gandhi was probably the first person in history to lift the love ethic of Jesus above mere interaction between individuals to a powerful and effective social force on a large scale. Love for Gandhi was a potent instrument for social and collective transformation. It was in this Gandhian emphasis on love and nonviolence that I discovered the method for social reform that I had been seeking for so many months. The intellectual and moral satisfaction that I failed to gain from the utilitarianism of Bentham and Mill, the revolutionary methods of Marx and Lenin, the social-contracts theory of Hobbes, the "back to nature" optimism of Rousseau, and the superman philosophy of Nietzsche, I found in the nonviolent resistance philosophy of Gandhi. I came to feel that this was the only morally and practically sound method open to oppressed people in their struggle for freedom.

But my intellectual odyssey to nonviolence did not end here. During my last year in theological school, I began to read the works of Reinhold Niebuhr. The prophetic and realistic elements in Niebuhr's passionate style and profound thought were appealing to me, and I became so enamored of his social ethics that I almost fell into the trap of accepting uncritically everything he wrote.

About this time I read Niebuhr's critique of the pacifist position. Niebuhr had himself once been a member of the pacifist ranks. For several years, he had been national chairman of the Fellowship of Reconciliation. His break with pacifism came in the early thirties, and the first full statement of his criticism of pacifism was in *Moral Man and Immoral Society*. Here he argued that there was no intrinsic moral difference between violent and nonviolent resistance. The social consequences of the two methods were different, he contended, but the differences were in degree rather than kind. Later Niebuhr began emphasizing the irresponsibility of relying on nonviolent resistance when there was no ground for believing that it would be successful in preventing the spread of totalitarian tyranny. It could only be successful, he argued, if the groups against whom the resistance was taking place had some degree of moral conscience, as was the case in Gandhi's struggle against the British. Niebuhr's ultimate rejection of pacifism was based primarily on the doctrine of man. He argued that pacifism failed to do justice to the reformation doctrine of justification by faith, substituting for it a sectarian perfectionism which believes "that divine grace actually lifts men out of the sinful contradictions of history and establishes him above the sins of the world."

At first, Niebuhr's critique of pacifism left me in a state of confusion. As I continued to read, however, I came to see more and more the shortcomings of his position. For instance, many of his statements revealed that he interpreted pacifism as a sort of passive nonresistance to evil expressing naïve trust in the power of love. But this was a serious distortion. My study of Gandhi convinced me that true pacifism is not nonresistance to evil, but nonviolent resistance to evil. Between the two positions, there is a world of difference. Gandhi resisted evil with as much vigor and power as the violent resister, but he resisted with love instead of hate. True pacifism is not unrealistic submission to evil power, as Niebuhr contends. It is rather a courageous confrontation of evil by the power of love, in the faith that it is better to be the recipient of violence than the inflicter of it, since the latter only multiplies the existence of violence and bitterness in the universe, while the former may develop a sense of shame in the opponent, and thereby bring about a transformation and change of heart.

In spite of the fact that I found many things to be desired in Niebuhr's philosophy, there were several points at which he constructively influenced my thinking. Niebuhr's great contribution to contemporary theology is that he has refuted the false optimism characteristic of a great segment of Protestant liberalism, without falling into the anti-rationalism of the continental theologian Karl Barth, or the semi-fundamentalism of other dialectical theologians. Moreover, Niebuhr has extraordinary insight into human nature, especially the behavior of nations and social groups. He is keenly aware of the complexity of human motives and of the relation between morality and power. His theology is a persistent reminder of the reality of sin on every level of man's existence. These elements in Niebuhr's thinking helped me to recognize the illusions of a superficial optimism concerning human nature and the dangers of a false idealism. While I still believed in man's potential for good, Niebuhr made me realize his potential for evil as well. Moreover, Niebuhr helped me to recognize the complexity of man's social involvement and the glaring reality of collective evil.

Many pacifists, I felt, failed to see this. All too many had an unwarranted optimism concerning man and leaned unconsciously toward self-righteousness. It was my revolt against these attitudes under the influence of Niebuhr that accounts for the fact that in spite of my strong leaning toward pacifism, I never joined a pacifist organization. After reading Niebuhr, I tried to arrive at a realistic pacifism. In other words, I came to see the pacifist position not as sinless but as the lesser evil in the circumstances. I felt then, and I feel now, that the pacifist would have a greater appeal if he did not claim to be free from the moral dilemmas that the Christian nonpacifist confronts.

The next stage of my intellectual pilgrimage to nonviolence came during my doctoral studies at Boston University. Here I had the opportunity to talk to many exponents of nonviolence, both students and visitors to the campus. Boston University School of Theology, under the influence of Dean Walter Muelder and Professor Allen Knight Chalmers, had a deep sympathy for pacifism. Both Dean Muelder and Dr. Chalmers had a passion for social justice that stemmed, not from a superficial optimism, but from a deep faith in the possibilities of human beings when they allowed themselves to become co-workers with God. It was at Boston University that I came to see that Niebuhr had over-emphasized the corruption of human nature. His pessimism concerning human nature was not balanced by an optimism concerning divine nature. He was so involved in diagnosing man's sickness of sin that he overlooked the cure of grace.

I studied philosophy and theology at Boston University under Edgar S. Brightman and L. Harold DeWolf. Both men greatly stimulated my thinking. It was mainly under these teachers that I studied personalistic philosophy—the theory that the clue to the meaning of ultimate reality is found in personality. This personal idealism remains today my basic philosophical position. Personalism's insistence that only personality—finite and infinite—is ultimately real strengthened me in two convictions: it gave me metaphysical and philosophical grounding for the idea of a personal God, and it gave me a metaphysical basis for the dignity and worth of all human personality.

Just before Dr. Brightman's death, I began studying the philosophy of Hegel with him. Although the course was mainly a study of Hegel's monumental work, *Phenomenology of Mind,* I spent my spare time reading his *Philosophy of History* and *Philosophy of Right.* There were points in Hegel's philosophy that I strongly disagreed with. For instance, his absolute idealism was rationally unsound to me because it tended to swallow up the many in the one. But there were other aspects of his thinking that I found stimulating. His contention that "truth is the whole" led me to a philosophical method of rational coherence. His analysis of the dialectical process, in spite of its shortcomings, helped me to see that growth comes through struggle.

In 1954 I ended my formal training with all of these relatively divergent intellectual forces converging into a positive social philosophy. One of the main tenets of this philosophy was the conviction that nonviolent resistance was one of the most potent weapons available to oppressed people in their quest for social justice. At this time, however, I had merely an intellectual understanding and appreciation of the position, with no firm determination to organize it in a socially effective situation.

When I went to Montgomery as a pastor, I had not the slightest idea that I would later become involved in a crisis in which nonviolent resistance would be applicable. I neither started the protest nor suggested it. I simply responded to the call of the people for a spokesman. When the protest began, my mind, consciously or unconsciously, was driven back to the Sermon on the Mount, with its sublime teachings on love, and the Gandhian method of nonviolent resistance. As the days unfolded, I came to see the power of nonviolence more and more. Living through the actual experience of the protest, nonviolence became more than a method to which I gave intellectual assent; it became a commitment to a way of life. Many of the things that I had not cleared up intellectually concerning nonviolence were now solved in the sphere of practical action.

Since the philosophy of nonviolence played such a positive role in the Montgomery Movement, it may be wise to turn to a brief discussion of some basic aspects of this philosophy.

First, it must be emphasized that nonviolent resistance is not a method for cowards; it does resist. If one uses this method because he is afraid or merely because he lacks the instruments of violence, he is not truly nonviolent. This is why Gandhi often said that if cowardice is the only alternative to violence, it is better to fight. He made this statement conscious of the fact that there is always another alternative: no individual or group need submit to any wrong, nor need they use violence to right the wrong; there is the way of nonviolence resistance. This is ultimately the way of the strong man. It is not a method of stagnant passivity. The phrase "passive resistance" often gives the false impression that this is a sort of "do-nothing method" in which the resister quietly and passively accepts evil. But nothing is further from the truth. For while the nonviolent resister is passive in the sense that he is not physically aggressive toward his opponent, his mind and emotions are always active, constantly seeking to persuade his opponent that he is wrong. The method is passive physically, but strongly active spiritually. It is not passive non-resistance to evil, it is active nonviolent resistance to evil.

A second basic fact that characterizes nonviolence is that it does not seek to defeat or humiliate the opponent, but to win his friendship and understanding. The nonviolent resister must often express his protest through noncoöperation or boycotts, but he realizes that these are not ends themselves; they are merely means to awaken a sense of moral shame in the opponent. The end is redemption and reconciliation. The aftermath of nonviolence is the creation of the beloved community, while the aftermath of violence is tragic bitterness.

A third characteristic of this method is that the attack is directed against forces of evil rather than against persons who happen to be doing the evil. It is evil that the nonviolent resister seeks to defeat, not the persons victimized by evil. If he is opposing racial injustice, the nonviolent resister has the vision to see that the basic tension is not between races. As I like to say to the people in Montgomery: "The tension in this city is not between white people and Negro people. The tension is, at bottom, between justice and injustice, between the forces of light and the forces of darkness. And if there is a victory, it will be a victory not merely for fifty thousand Negroes, but a victory for justice and the forces of light. We are out to defeat injustice and not white persons who may be unjust."

A fourth point that characterizes nonviolent resistance is a willingness to accept suffering without retaliation, to accept blows from the opponent without striking back. "Rivers of blood may have to flow before we gain our freedom, but it must be our blood," Gandhi said to his countrymen. The nonviolent resister is willing to accept violence if necessary, but never to inflict it. He does not seek to dodge jail. If going to jail is necessary, he enters it "as a bridegroom enters the bride's chamber."

One may well ask: "What is the nonviolent resister's justification for this ordeal to which he invites men, for this mass political application of the ancient doctrine of turning the other cheek?" The answer is found in the realization that unearned suffering is redemptive. Suffering, the nonviolent resister realizes, has tremendous educational and transforming possibilities. "Things of fundamental importance to people are not secured by reason alone, but have to be purchased with their suffering," said Gandhi. He continues: "Suffering is infinitely more powerful than the law of the jungle for converting the opponent and opening his ears which are otherwise shut to the voice of reason."

A fifth point concerning nonviolent resistance is that it avoids not only external physical violence but also internal violence of spirit. The nonviolent resister not only refuses to shoot his opponent but he also refuses to hate him. At the center of nonviolence stands the principle of love. The nonviolent resister would contend that in the struggle for human dignity, the oppressed people of the world must not succumb to the temptation of becoming bitter or indulging in hate campaigns. To retaliate in kind would do nothing but intensify the existence of hate in the universe. Along the way of life, someone must have sense enough and morality enough to cut off the chain of hate. This can only be done by projecting the ethic of love to the center of our lives.

In speaking of love at this point, we are not referring to some sentimental or affectionate emotion. It would be nonsense to urge men to love their oppressors in an affectionate sense. Love in this connection means understanding, redemptive good will. Here the Greek language comes to our aid. There are three words for love in the Greek New Testament. First, there is *eros*. In Platonic philosophy *eros* meant the yearning of the soul for the realm of the divine. It has come now to mean a sort of aesthetic or romantic love. Second, there is *philia* which means intimate affection between personal friends. *Philia* denotes a sort of reciprocal love; the person loves because he is loved. When we speak of loving those who oppose us, we refer to neither *eros* nor *philia;* we speak of a love which is expressed in the Greek word *agape. Agape* means understanding, redeeming good will for all men. It is an overflowing love which is purely spontaneous, unmotivated, groundless, and creative. It is not set in motion by any quality or function of its object. It is the love of God operating in the human heart.

Agape is disinterested love. It is a love in which the individual seeks not his own good, but the good of his neighbor (I Cor. 10:24). *Agape* does not begin by discriminating between worthy and unworthy people, or any qualities people possess. It begins by loving others *for their sakes*. It is an entirely "neighbor-regarding concern for others," which discovers the neighbor in every man it meets. Therefore, *agape* makes no distinction between friend and enemy; it is directed toward both. If one loves an individual merely on account of his friendliness, he loves him for the sake of the benefits to be gained from the friendship, rather than for the friend's own sake. Consequently, the best way to assure oneself that Love is disinterested is to have love for the enemy-neighbor from whom you can expect no good in return, but only hostility and persecution.

Another basic point about *agape* is that it springs from the *need* of the other person—his need for belonging to the best in the human family. The Samaritan who helped the Jew on the Jericho Road was "good" because he responded to the human need that he was presented with. God's love is eternal and fails not because man needs his love. St. Paul assures us that the loving act of redemption was done "while we were yet sinners"—that is, at the point of our greatest need for love. Since the white man's personality is greatly distorted by segregation, and his soul is greatly scarred, he needs the love of the Negro. The Negro must love the white man, because the white man needs his love to remove his tensions, insecurities, and fears.

Agape is not a weak, passive love. It is love in action. *Agape* is love seeking to preserve and create community. It is insistence on community even when one seeks to break it. *Agape* is a willingness to sacrifice in the interest of mutuality. *Agape* is a willingness to go to any length to restore community. It doesn't stop at the first mile, but it goes the second mile to restore community. It is a willingness to forgive, not seven times, but seventy times seven to restore community. The cross is the eternal expression of the length to which God will go in order to restore broken community. The resurrection is a symbol of God's triumph over all the forces that seek to block community. The Holy Spirit is the

continuing community creating reality that moves through history.
He who works against community is working against the whole
of creation. Therefore, if I respond to hate with a reciprocal hate
I do nothing but intensify the cleavage in broken community. I
can only close the gap in broken community by meeting hate with
love. If I meet hate with hate, I become depersonalized, because
creation is so designed that my personality can only be fulfilled
in the context of community. Booker T. Washington was right:
"Let no man pull you so low as to make you hate him." When he
pulls you that low he brings you to the point of working against
community; he drags you to the point of defying creation, and
thereby becoming depersonalized.

In the final analysis, *agape* means a recognition of the fact that
all life is interrelated. All humanity is involved in a single process,
and all men are brothers. To the degree that I harm my brother,
no matter what he is doing to me, to that extent I am harming
myself. For example, white men often refuse federal aid to education in order to avoid giving the Negro his rights; but because
all men are brothers they cannot deny Negro children without
harming their own. They end, all efforts to the contrary, by hurt-
ing themselves. Why is this? Because men are brothers. If you
harm me, you harm yourself.

Love, *agape*, is the only cement that can hold this broken community together. When I am commanded to love, I am commanded to restore community, to resist injustice, and to meet the
needs of my brothers.

A sixth basic fact about nonviolent resistance is that it is based
on the conviction that the universe is on the side of justice. Consequently, the believer in nonviolence has deep faith in the
future. This faith is another reason why the nonviolent resister
can accept suffering without retaliation. For he knows that in
his struggle for justice he has cosmic companionship. It is true

that there are devout believers in nonviolence who find it difficult to believe in a personal God. But even these persons believe in the existence of some creative force that works for universal wholeness. Whether we call it an unconscious process, an impersonal Brahman, or a Personal Being of matchless power and infinite love, there is a creative force in this universe that works to bring the disconnected aspects of reality into a harmonious whole.

VII

Methods of the Opposition

IN SPITE of the fact that the bus protest had been an immediate success, the city fathers—three in number, including the mayor—and the bus officials felt that it would fizzle out in a few days. They were certain that the first rainy day would find the Negroes back on the buses. Guided by this expectation, they refused to make any move toward the Negro community to determine what conditions needed to be met in order to rectify the situation. But the first rainy day came and passed and the buses remained empty.

In the meantime, the city fathers and the bus officials had expressed their first willingness to negotiate. Late Wednesday afternoon, December 7, Rev. Robert Hughes, executive director of the Alabama Council on Human Relations, called to say that he and two other members of the council—Rev. Thomas P. Thrasher, white rector of one of the leading Episcopal churches of the city, and Dr. H. Councill Trenholm, president of Alabama State College—had succeeded in getting the city fathers to consent to a meeting with the Negro leaders and the bus officials the next morning at eleven o'clock.

At a special session of the MIA executive board a negotiating committee of twelve was appointed* and I was chosen to serve as their spokesman. It was agreed that we would present to the

* See Appendix.

108

meeting the same three proposals that had been adopted on the preceding Monday night: briefly, (1) a guarantee of courteous treatment; (2) passengers to be seated on a first-come first-served basis, the Negroes seating from the back; and (3) employment of Negro bus operators on predominantly Negro routes. The aim of these proposals was frankly no more than a temporary alleviation of the problem that we confronted. We never felt that the first-come first-served seating arrangement would provide a final solution, since this would eventually have to depend on a change in the law. We were sure, however, that the Rosa Parks case, which was now in the courts, provided the test that would ultimately bring about the defeat of bus segregation itself.

We arrived at the city hall about fifteen minutes before the hour set for the meeting. There we were directed to the Commissioners' Chamber, a room of moderate size, with the commissioners' table at one end and chairs arranged in front of it. We sat down near the front, and soon Thrasher, Hughes, and Trenholm came in and joined us. Two or three reporters were on hand and television cameras emphasized the importance of the occasion. Promptly at eleven the three commissioners—Mayor W. A. Gayle, Commissioner Clyde Sellers, and Commissioner Frank A. Parks—filed in and sat at the table facing us. They were joined by J. E. Bagley and Jack Crenshaw, representing the bus company, who took seats near one end of the table. Thus the lines appeared to be clearly drawn before the meeting began.

The mayor called the meeting to order, and invited Mr. Thrasher to make the opening statement. Thrasher—a man deeply dedicated to the ideal of Christian brotherhood—came to the front of the room and briefly presented the reasons why the Council on Human Relations had requested the meeting. He went on to express his faith in the ability of both sides to be reasonable and unemotional in all of the deliberations.

The mayor then turned to the Negro delegation and demanded: "Who is the spokesman?" When all eyes turned toward me, the mayor said: "All right, come forward and make your statement." In the glare of the television lights, I walked slowly toward the front of the room and took a seat at the opposite end of the table from Bagley and Crenshaw.

I opened by stating briefly why we found it necessary to "boycott" the buses. I made it clear that the arrest of Mrs. Parks was not the cause of the protest, but merely the precipitating factor. "Our action," I said, "is the culmination of a series of injustices and indignities that have existed over the years." I went on to cite many instances of discourtesy on the part of the bus drivers, and numerous occasions when Negro passengers had had to stand over empty seats. I emphasized that the Negroes had shown a great deal of patience, and had attempted to negotiate around the conference table on several occasions before to no avail.

After these background remarks I set forth the three requests and proceeded to explain each proposal in detail. I made it clear, for instance, that our request for a first-come, first-served seating arrangement, with Negroes loading from the back and whites from the front, was not something totally new for the South; other Southern cities—such as Nashville, Atlanta, and even Mobile, Alabama—followed this pattern, and each of them adhered as rigorously to a pattern of segregation as did Montgomery. As far as the request for a guarantee of courtesy from the drivers was concerned, "this is the least that any business can grant to its patrons," I said. And finally I pointed out that since the Negroes poured so much money into the pocketbook of the bus company, it was only fair for some of it to be returned to them in the form of jobs as operators on predominately Negro routes. "The bus company admits," I reminded them, "that seventy-five per cent of its patrons are colored; and it seems to me that it would be good business sense for the company to seek employees from the ranks of its largest patronage." I closed my remarks by assuring the commissioners that we planned to conduct the protest on the highest level of dignity and restraint, and I avowed that our aim was not to put the bus company out of business, but to achieve justice for ourselves as well as for the white man.

As soon as I finished the mayor opened the meeting to general discussion. Several members of the Negro delegation further elaborated on the three proposals. Then the commissioners and the attorney for the bus company began raising questions. They challenged the legality of the seating arrangement that we were proposing. They contended that the Negroes were demanding something that would violate the law. We answered by reiterating our previous argument that a first-come first-served seating arrangement could exist entirely within the segregation law, as it did in many Southern cities.

It soon became clear that Crenshaw, the attorney for the bus company, was our most stubborn opponent. Doggedly he sought to convince the group that there was no way to grant the suggested seating proposal without violating the city ordinance. The more Crenshaw talked, the more he won the city fathers to his position. Mayor Gayle and Commissioner Sellers became more and more intransigent. Eventually I saw that the meeting was getting nowhere, and suggested that we bring it to a close. Thereupon the mayor asked a few members of the Negro delegation to stay over with the officials of the bus company, in an attempt to come to some settlement.

As soon as the others had left we assembled around the conference table with Bagley, Crenshaw, and the two associate commissioners—Sellers and Parks. In the smaller group, with the press no longer recording every word, it seemed possible that some progress could at last be made. Soon after we had restated our position on seating, I heard Commissioner Parks say in a quiet voice,

"I don't see why we can't arrange to accept this seating proposal. We can work it within our segregation laws."

My hopes began to rise. But Parks had hardly closed his mouth before Crenshaw rejoined,

"But, Frank. I don't see how we can do it within the law. If it were legal I would be the first to go along with it; but it just isn't legal. The only way that it can be done is to change your segregation laws."

This put a quick end to my optimism. Lacking the resolution to stand firm on his conviction, Parks was readily dissuaded. Finally Crenshaw revealed the basis of his propostion:

"If we granted the Negroes these demands," he asserted, "they would go about boasting of a victory that they had won over the white people; and this we will not stand for."

Now, at least, Crenshaw's motives were out in the open. We tried to convince him that the Negroes had no such intention. We assured him that if the proposals were granted we would make it our primary business to restrain our people from proclaiming their victory. But none of these assurances moved him. Seeing the futility of continuing, I finally asked him to state specifically what the bus company would be willing to offer the Negroes. His answer was brief: "We will certainly be willing to guarantee courtesy. But we cannot change the seating arrangement because such a change would violate the law. And as far as bus drivers are concerned, we have no intention now or in the foreseeable future of hiring 'niggras.'"

Four hours of deliberation had come to an end without settlement.

I left the meeting despondent, but I soon saw that I was the victim of an unwarranted pessimism because I had started out with an unwarranted optimism. I had gone to the meeting with a great illusion. Feeling that our demands were moderate, I had assumed that they would be granted with little question; I had believed that the privileged would give up their privileges on request. This experience, however, taught me a lesson. I came to see that no one gives up his privileges without strong resistance. I saw further that the underlying purpose of segregation was to oppress and exploit the segregated, not simply to keep them apart. Even when we asked for justice *within* the segregation laws, the "powers that be" were not willing to grant it. Justice and equality, I saw, would never come while segregation remained, because the basic purpose of segregation was to perpetuate injustice and inequality.

Shortly after this first negotiating conference, I called a meeting of the executive board of the MIA to report the results. The members were disappointed, but agreed that we should stand firm on our three proposals. By this time someone had discovered that the Montgomery City Lines were owned by a company with headquarters in Chicago; this company—National City Lines, Inc.—operated buses in more than thirty-five cities. It was agreed that we should wire the president of the National City Lines stating our grievances, and urging him to come immediately, or send a representative, to Montgomery to negotiate further. Two days later the president replied that one of the company vice-presidents would be down in two or three days.

This favorable response gave us new hope, and we waited patiently for the representative from Chicago. After several days had passed and I had heard nothing, I began to wonder whether the company had backed out. In this state of uncertainty I received a call from one of my white friends on the morning of

December 15, saying that he had heard from reliable sources that a Mr. C. K. Totten was in town from the National City Lines, and wondering whether I had talked to him. When I answered with obvious disappointment, my friend offered to check further. Sure enough, in about two hours he called me back to say that Totten was definitely in Montgomery and had been around for two or three days. It seemed strange to me that the bus official had been in town this long without trying to speak to anyone in the MIA, but I continued to wait for his call. The wait was in vain. I never heard from Mr. Totten.

In the meantime, the mayor sent word that he was calling a citizens committee to meet with the bus officials and Negro leaders on the morning of December 17. Over a week had passed since the first conference and the protest had still shown no signs of faltering.

The executive board of the MIA once more met to discuss our position. Again we agreed to stand firm on the three proposals. There was, however, this slight modification of the third point: considering the possibility that there were no imminent vacancies and taking into account the existence of certain priorities due to union regulations, it was agreed that we would not demand the immediate hiring of Negro bus drivers, but would settle for the willingness of the bus company to take applications from Negroes and hire some as soon as vacancies occurred.

Only a few people had assembled when we entered the conference room on Saturday morning, and these seemed exceptionally cordial. One of the first who came forward to greet us was Rev. Henry E. Russell, minister of the Trinity Presbyterian Church of Montgomery and brother of Senator Richard Russell of Georgia. I remember the heartiness of his smile and the warmth of his handclasp. Gradually, others came and they, too, appeared friendly. We began to hope that something better might come of this second meeting.

Just before the meeting opened I noticed an unfamiliar man entering the room with Bagley and Crenshaw. He was introduced as C. K. Totten of Chicago. He greeted each of us warmly, but said nothing of why he had not been in touch with our group. I also noticed two Negro citizens who were not on the committee appointed to represent the Negro community. I soon discovered that they were there on special invitation from the mayor. This made me rather suspicious of what was going on.

Finally, the mayor came in, followed by the two associate commissioners. By this time all were present: the three commissioners; four representatives from the bus company; the committee representing the Negro community; the two Negro men invited by the mayor; and the mayor's citizens committee, among them the Revs. Henry Parker, then minister of First Baptist Church, E. Stanley Frazier, then minister of St. James Methodist Church, and Henry Russell.

After summarizing the situation, the mayor called upon me to explain the Negroes' proposals. When I had finished he called on a representative from the bus company, and C. K. Totten rose to his feet.

As Totten stood up before the group I waited anxiously to hear what he would say. Because he came from outside, there was always a possibility that he would see the problem in a different light from his associates. Slowly and deliberately he spoke of each of our proposals. As he took them up one by one no doubt remained: he was taking the same position that the city commission and Crenshaw had held in the first meeting. If Totten could have miraculously acquired a Southern accent, and spoken without

being seen, I would have sworn that he was Jack Crenshaw. I
knew then that he had been "brainwashed" by the city commission and the bus officials.

As Totten continued, my indignation grew. I reflected bitterly
that he had not even given the Negroes the courtesy of a hearing,
in spite of the fact that we were the ones who had invited him
to Montgomery. This was a difficult moment. Should I challenge
his biased and one-sided presentation or let it pass? The question
turned over and over in my mind. When he had finished, things
were quiet for a moment. Then unable to restrain myself any
longer I jumped to my feet and gave voice to my resentment: "Mr.
Totten has not been fair in his assertions. He has made a statement that is completely biased. In spite of the fact that he was
asked to come to Montgomery by the MIA, he has not done the
Negro community the simple courtesy of hearing their grievances.
The least that all of us can do in our deliberations is to be honest
and fair." A chorus of amens could be heard from the Negro
delegation. Neither the mayor nor C. K. Totten replied, but the
latter shifted uncomfortably in his seat.

The meeting proceeded with statements from several of the
citizens who had been invited by the mayor. I remember especially the words of Dr. Frazier—one of the most outspoken segregationists in the Methodist Church. Although I had heard his
name and read his segregationist statements, I had never been
in his presence. Now I saw a tall, distinguished-looking man, the
quintessence of dignity. He was, I soon found, articulate and eloquent besides. He talked persuasively about the frailties and
weaknesses of human nature. He made it clear that he felt the
Negroes were wrong in boycotting the buses; and the even greater
wrong, he contended, lay in the fact that the protest was being
led by ministers of the gospel. The job of the minister, he averred,
is to lead the souls of men to God, not to bring about confusion

by getting tangled up in transitory social problems. He moved on to a brief discussion of the Christmas story. In evocative terms he talked of "God's unspeakable gift." He ended by saying that as we moved into the Christmas season, our minds and hearts should be turned toward the Babe of Bethlehem; and he urged the Negro ministers to leave the meeting determined to bring this boycott to a close and lead their people instead "to a glorious experience of the Christian faith."

Again I felt the need of answering. "We too know the Jesus that the minister just referred to," I said. "We have had an experience with him, and we believe firmly in the revelation of God in Jesus Christ. I can see no conflict between our devotion to Jesus Christ and our present action. In fact I see a necessary relationship. If one is truly devoted to the religion of Jesus he will seek to rid the earth of social evils. The gospel is social as well as personal. We are only doing in a minor way what Gandhi did in India; and certainly no one referred to him as an unrepentant sinner; he is considered by many a saint.

"We have been talking a great deal this morning about customs," I concluded. "It has been affirmed that any change in present conditions would mean going against the 'cherished customs' of our community. But if the customs are wrong we have every reason in the world to change them. The decision which we must make now is whether we will give our allegiance to outmoded and unjust customs or to the ethical demands of the universe. As Christians we owe our ultimate allegiance to God and His will, rather than to man and his folkways."

After a few more people had spoken, the mayor announced that he would appoint a small group from the citizens committee to meet with representatives from the MIA and the bus company. These groups were to work out some settlement and bring it back to him in the form of a recommendation. At first the mayor tried to stack the committee by appointing eight white people from the citizens committee, the two Negro men whom he had invited personally, and only three people from the MIA. But Jo Ann Robinson immediately took issue, insisting that the only equitable way to handle the problem was to appoint as many Negroes as whites. Thereupon the mayor reluctantly raised the number of Negroes to eight. He appointed Rev. Henry Parker chairman.

After the larger group had left the room, and Parker had called the new committee to order, Frazier asked permission to read a suggested solution to the seating problem. Its substance was that signs be placed on the buses clearly stating the section for each race to occupy. No more than ten spaces would be reserved for either race. In the event that whites or Negroes completely filled the seats in their section, the vacant seats beyond their prescribed area could be temporarily occupied so long as members of the opposite race did not board the bus. The members of the Negro group instantly rejected this idea, finding the idea of racial signs repugnant, and believing that acceptance would mean a step backward rather than forward.

Several of the white committeemen then suggested that we return to the buses, and come back after the Christmas holidays to work out a settlement. They contended that the white community would listen more sympathetically to our requests if we first called off the protest. Our response was again negative. We felt that all of our efforts would have been in vain if we called off the protest simply with the promise that something might be done about conditions later. By now considerable time had passed, and the chairman suggested that we adjourn and reassemble on Monday morning at ten.

At the close of the meeting I had my first opportunity to talk face to face with Totten. Almost sheepishly he admitted that the plan we were offering was the one followed by the Mobile City

Lines—another company owned by the National City Lines, Inc. "And as far as I am concerned," he said, "it would work very well in Montgomery. But the city commission seems to feel that it will not be acceptable." I was tempted to ask why he hadn't had the courage to say this in the general meeting when the commissioners were present, but I restrained myself, and the conversation ended on a friendly note.

As I drove home my mind went back to Frazier and his eloquence. How firmly he believed in the position he was taking. He would probably never change now; time-worn traditions had become too crystallized in his soul. The "isness" of segregation had for him become one with the "oughtness" of the moral law. Yet even though I totally disagreed with his point of view, and knew that history and religion had proven him wrong, I admired his sincerity and zeal. Why is it, I asked myself, that the whites who believe in integration are so often less eloquent, less positive, in their testimony than the segregationists? It is still one of the tragedies of human history that the "children of darkness" are frequently more determined and zealous than the "children of light."

Sunday, December 18, rolled away. At ten o'clock Monday morning we reassembled to continue our deliberations. Everyone was on hand and Parker was again presiding. Just after the meeting was called to order, I noticed a man who had not been present on Saturday and who, as far as I could remember, had not been appointed to the eight-man citizens committee by the Mayor. Someone next to me whispered, "That is Luther Ingalls—secretary of the Montgomery White Citizens Council."

As soon as the discussion period opened Ingalls stood up to make a statement. I immediately jumped to the floor and challanged his right to speak since he was not a member of the committee. "Furthermore," I continued, "we will never solve this problem so long as there are persons on the committee whose public pronouncements are anti-Negro."

At this Dr. Parker replied angrily: "He has just as much right to be on this committee as you do. You have a definite point of view and you are on it."

Thereupon the other white members of the committee began to lash out against me. They contended that I was the chief stumbling block to a real solution of the problem. A Mrs. Hipp said vehemently that I had insulted her by implying that she, along with other white members of the committee, had come to the meeting with a closed mind. I tried to make it clear that my statement applied only to those people whose public pronouncements were anti-Negro, and not to the committee as a whole, but to no avail. They continued to look at me as though I were the cause of the stalemate.

For a moment it appeared that I was alone. Nobody came to my rescue, until suddenly Ralph Abernathy was on the floor in my defense. He insisted that I spoke for the whole Negro delegation. He pointed out that since I was the spokesman for the group I naturally had to do most of the talking, but this did not mean that I did not have the support of the rest of the committee. As he continued, one could see obvious disappointment on the faces of the white committee members. By trying to convince the Negroes that I was the main obstacle to a solution they had hoped to divide us among ourselves. But Ralph's statement left no doubt. From this moment on the white group saw the futility of attempting to negotiate us into a compromise. A few more questions were raised and a few more suggestions were made; whereupon Parker brought the meeting to a close, promising to call another one later. But the other meeting was never called.

That Monday I went home with a heavy heart. I was weighted

down by a terrible sense of guilt, remembering that on two or three occasions I had allowed myself to become angry and indignant. I had spoken hastily and resentfully. Yet I knew that this was no way to solve a problem. "You must not harbor anger," I admonished myself. "You must be willing to suffer the anger of the opponent, and yet not return anger. You must not become bitter. No matter how emotional your opponents are, you must be calm."

In this mood I went to the telephone and called Parker. He was obviously surprised to hear my voice. I told him that I was sorry about the misunderstanding that had come up in the meeting, and wanted to apologize if I was in any way responsible. He responded by seeking to justify the position he had taken. This led him into a discussion of the race problem in general and the bus situation in particular. He was certain that the Negroes had no basic justification for boycotting the buses, "since many white persons are treated just as discourteously as Negroes." As far as the general problem was concerned, he felt that Negroes all over were pushing things too fast, and this, he contended, could lead to nothing but trouble. I thanked him for talking to me, and the conversation ended.

One further attempt was made to reopen negotiations, thanks to the good offices of another group of white citizens. The Men of Montgomery was an organization composed of the most influential businessmen of the city. They had already begun to see the effects of the protest on trade, and realized that a prolonged conflict could be disastrous. Moreover, their leaders were men of good will who abhorred the increasing tension they saw around them. This is not to imply that these men were stanch integrationists; far from it. Some of them believed firmly in segregation, and even those who did not would probably have agreed with Parker that the Negroes were "pushing things too fast." But at

least they were open-minded enough to listen to another point
of view and discuss the problem of race intelligently. Twice, a half
a dozen of the Men of Montgomery met with a similar number
from the MIA in an earnest effort to settle the protest, and I have
no doubt that we would have come to a solution had it not been
for the recalcitrance of the city commission. As it was, our joint
effort petered out with no results.

After the opposition had failed to negotiate us into a compromise, it turned to subtler means for blocking the protest;
namely, to conquer by dividing. False rumors were spread concerning the leaders of the movement. Negro workers were told
by their white employers that their leaders were only concerned
with making money out of the movement. Others were told
that the Negro leaders rode big cars while they walked. During
this period the rumor was spread that I had purchased a brand
new Cadillac for myself and a Buick station wagon for my wife.
Of course none of this was true.

Not only was there a conscious attempt to raise questions about
the integrity of the Negro leaders, and thereby cause their followers to lose faith in them; there was also an attempt to divide
the leaders among themselves. Prominent white citizens went to
many of the older Negro ministers and said: "If there has to be a
protest, you should be the leaders. It is a shame for you, who have
been in the community for so many years, to have your own
people overlook you and choose these young upstarts to lead
them." Certain members of the white community tried to convince several of the other protest leaders that the problem could
be solved if I were out of the picture. "If one of you," they
would say, "took over the leadership, things would change overnight."

I almost broke down under the continual battering of this argument. I began to think that there might be some truth in it, and I also feared that some were being influenced by this argument. After two or three troubled days and nights of little sleep, I called a meeting of the executive board and offered my resignation. I told them that I would be the last person to want to stand in the way of a solution to the problem which plagued our community, and that maybe a more mature person could bring about a speedier conclusion. I suggested the names of two men who had worked closely with me and whose competence no one could question. I further assured the board that I would be as active in the background as I had been in the position of spokesman. But I had barely finished talking before board members began to urge me from every side to forget the idea of resignation. With a unanimous vote of confidence, they made it clear that they were well pleased with the way I was handling things, and that they would follow my leadership to the end.

Afterward, as I drove up to the parsonage, more at peace than I had been in some time, I could hear Coretta's high, true soprano through the living room window. In the back bedroom "Yoki," now more than a month old, was wide awake and busy discovering her fingers. I picked her up and walked to the front room, bouncing her in time to Coretta's song.

Such moments together had become rare. We could never plan them, for I seldom knew from one hour to the next when I would be home. Many times Coretta saw her good meals grow dry in the oven when a sudden emergency kept me away. Yet she never complained, and she was always there when I needed her. "Yoki" and Beethoven, she said, kept her company when she was alone. Calm and unruffled, Coretta moved quietly about the business of keeping the household going. When I needed to talk things out, she was ready to listen, or to offer suggestions when I asked for them. Her fortitude was my strength. Afraid for me at times, she never allowed her fears to worry me or impede my work in the protest. And she seemed to have no fear for herself. Several times, in the months that followed, I sent her and "Yoki" to Atlanta to stay with my parents, or to Marion to stay with hers. But she never stayed long. "When I am away from this," she told a reporter, "I feel depressed and helpless." And so time and again she was back ahead of schedule.

The height of the attempt to conquer by dividing came on Sunday, January 22, when the city commissioners shocked the Negro community by announcing in the local newspaper that they had met with a group of prominent Negro ministers and worked out a settlement. The terms of the so-called "settlement" were: (1) a guarantee of courtesy; (2) a white reserved section at the front of the bus, and a Negro reserved section at the rear, with first-come, first-served obtaining for the unreserved, middle section; (3) special, all-Negro buses during the rush hours. Actually, except for the first provision, this "settlement" was nothing but a restatement of conditions that had existed prior to the protest. At some points it was a backward step. Nevertheless, many people were convinced the boycott was over.

It was soon clear that this announcement was a calculated design to get the Negroes back on the buses Sunday morning. The city commission felt certain that once a sizable number of Negroes began riding the buses, the boycott would end.

We were able to stave off the effects of this announcement by a set of interesting circumstances. Although the *Montgomery Advertiser* had apparently agreed to hold the story until Sunday morning, the Associated Press sent it out on Saturday evening. Carl T. Rowan, Negro editorial writer of the *Minneapolis Tribune*, caught the story as it came over the wires, and was amazed to learn that the Negroes had settled for such a "half loaf." Mr.

Rowan had been to Montgomery a few weeks before to cover the boycott, and had established a close relationship with the MIA leaders. Around eight o'clock on Saturday evening, he called me long distance to verify the story. When he mentioned the meeting and settlement I was astonished, and when he spoke of three prominent Negro ministers present at the meeting I was even more puzzled. I told him that I knew nothing about the matter, and I began to wonder whether any of my associates had betrayed me and made an agreement in my absence. "But this can't be true," I said, "because I was in a strategy meeting this morning, and all of the 'prominent ministers' were there."

Rowan agreed to call Commissioner Sellers and get more detailed information. In about twenty minutes he phoned back to say that Sellers had confirmed the story but refused to give the names of the "prominent Negro ministers." Rowan had been able, however, to get their denominations from the commissioner. This clue was all I needed.

I asked several of my associates to come to my house immediately, and in less than thirty minutes they were all there. I told them the story, and we determined to get at the root of it before midnight. First we needed to find out if a group of Negro ministers had actually met with the city commission. Remembering the denominations that Rowan had mentioned, we started to track the identities down by a process of elimination. After about an hour of calling here and there we were able to identify the "three prominent Negro ministers." They were neither prominent nor were they members of the MIA.

It was now about eleven o'clock on Saturday night. Something had to be done to let the people know that the article they would read the next morning was false. I asked one group to call all the Negro ministers of the city and urge them to announce in church Sunday morning that the protest was still on. Another group joined me on a tour of the Negro night clubs and taverns to inform those present of the false settlement. For the first time I had a chance to see the inside of most of Montgomery's night spots. At one o'clock Sunday morning we were still making the announcement in clubs. As a result of our fast maneuvering, the word got around so well that the next day the buses were empty as usual.

I soon had a chance to talk to each of the "three prominent Negro ministers" personally. To a man they insisted that they had not agreed on any settlement. They asserted that they had been "hoodwinked" into the conference on the basis of a telephone invitation to join in a discussion of a new type of insurance for the city. All three publicly repudiated the commission's announcement.

With the failure of the attempted hoax, the city fathers lost face. Not only had they been outmaneuvered, but their veracity had been challenged. They were now desperate. Their answer was to embark on a "get-tough" policy. In obvious indignation, the mayor went on television and denounced the boycott. He threatened that the commission was going to "stop pussy-footing around with the boycott." The vast majority of white Montgomerians, he declared, did not care if a Negro ever rode the buses again, and he called upon the white employers to stop driving Negro employees to and from work. During this period all three city commissioners let it be known that they had joined the White Citizens Council.

The "get-tough" policy turned out to be a series of arrests for minor and often imaginary traffic violations. People who had never received a ticket were booked, and on several occasions taken to jail. Negro drivers in the car pool were stopped throughout the city and questioned about their licenses, their insurance, their place of work. The policemen made careful notes, apparently in the hope of building up subsequent cases. Some ex-bus riders, waiting to be picked up, were told that there was a law against hitchhiking; others were told that they would be arrested for vagrancy if they were found "milling around white neighborhoods."

Faced with these difficulties, the volunteer car pool began to weaken. Some drivers became afraid that their licenses would be revoked or their insurance canceled; others felt that they could no longer adhere to nonviolence under such circumstances. Many of the drivers quietly dropped out of the pool. It became more and more difficult to catch a ride. Complaints began to rise. From early morning to late at night my telephone rang and my doorbell was seldom silent. I began to have doubts about the ability of the Negro community to continue the struggle.

In an attempt to keep things together the ministers made special appeals at mass meetings, urging the people to stand fast. We assured the drivers in the car pool that we would stick with them through their difficulties. "We must remain together," we kept repeating, "for better or for worse, until this problem is solved."

I did not suspect that I myself was soon to face arrest as a result of the "get-tough" operation. One afternoon in the middle of January, after several hours of work at my church office, I started driving home with a friend, Robert Williams, and the church secretary, Mrs. Lilie Thomas. Before leaving the downtown district I decided to make a quick trip to the parking lot to pick up a few people going in my direction. As we entered the lot, I noticed four or five policemen questioning the drivers. I picked up three passengers and drove to the edge of the lot, where I was stopped by one of these officers. While he was asking to see my license and questioning me concerning the ownership of the car, I heard a policeman across the street say, "That's that damn King fellow."

Leaving the lot, I noticed two motorcycle policemen behind me. One was still following three blocks later. When I told Bob Williams that we were being trailed, he said, "Be sure that you follow every traffic regulation." Slowly and meticulously I drove toward home, with the motorcycle behind me. Finally, as I stopped to let the three passengers out, the policeman pulled up and said: "Get out, King; you are under arrest for speeding thirty miles an hour in a twenty-five mile zone." Without a question I got out of the car, telling Bob Williams and Mrs. Thomas to drive on and notify my wife. Soon a patrol car came, two policemen got out and searched me from top to bottom, put me in the car, and drove off.

As we drove off, presumably to the city jail, a feeling of panic began to come over me. I had always had the impression that the jail was in the downtown section of Montgomery. Yet after riding for a while I noticed that we were going in a different direction. The more we rode the farther we were from the center of town. In a few minutes we turned into a dark and dingy street that I had never seen and headed under a desolate old bridge. By this time I was convinced that these men were carrying me to some faraway spot to dump me off. "But this couldn't be," I said to myself. "These men are officers of the law." Then I began to wonder whether they were driving me out to some waiting mob, planning to use the excuse later on that they had been over-powered. I found myself trembling within and without. Silently, I asked God to give me the strength to endure whatever came.

By this time we were passing under the bridge. I was sure now that I was going to meet my fateful hour on the other side. But as I looked up I noticed a glaring light in the distance, and soon I saw the words "Montgomery City Jail." I was so relieved that it was some time before I realized the irony of my position: going to jail at that moment seemed like going to some safe haven!

A policeman ushered me in. After depositing my things and giving the jailer the desired information, I was led to a dingy and odorous cell. As the big iron door swung open the jailer said to me: "All right, get on in there with all the others." For the moment strange gusts of emotion swept through me like cold winds on an open prairie. For the first time in my life I had been thrown behind bars.

As I entered the crowded cell, I recognized two acquaintances, one a teacher, who had also been arrested on pretexts connected with the protest. In the democracy of the jail they were packed together with vagrants and drunks and serious lawbreakers. One cellmate was in on a charge of assault and battery; another stood accused of collecting funds under false pretenses. But the democracy did not go so far as to break the rules of segregation. Here whites and Negroes languished in separate enclosures.

When I began to look around I was so appalled at the conditions I saw that I soon forgot my own predicament. I saw men lying on hard wood slats, and others resting on cots with torn-up mattresses. The toilet was in one corner of the cell without a semblance of an enclosure. I said to myself that no matter what these men had done, they shouldn't be treated like this.

They all gathered around to find out why I was there, and showed some surprise that the city had gone so far as to arrest me. Soon one man after another began talking to me about his reason for being in jail and asking if I could help him get out. After the third person had asked my help, I turned to the group and said: "Fellows, before I can assist in getting any of you out, I've got to get my ownself out." At this they laughed.

Shortly after, the jailer came to get me. As I left the cell, wondering where he was going to take me, one of the men called after me: "Don't forget us when you get out." I assured them that I would not forget. The jailer led me down a long corridor into a little room in the front of the jail. I thought for a moment that I was going to be bonded out, but I soon discovered my mistake. Curtly the jailer ordered me to be seated, and began rubbing my fingers on an ink pad. I was about to be fingerprinted like a criminal.

By this time the news of my arrest had spread over Montgomery, and a number of people had headed for the city jail. The first to arrive was my good friend Ralph Abernathy. He immediately sought to sign my bond, but the officials told him that he had to bring a certified statement from the court asserting that he owned a sufficient amount of property to sign a bond. Ralph pointed out that since it was almost six-thirty at night, the courthouse was already closed.

Indifferently, the official retorted: "Well, you will just have to wait till tomorrow morning."

Ralph then asked if he could see me.

The jailer replied: "No, you can't see him until ten o'clock tomorrow."

"Well, is it possible," said Abernathy, "to pay a cash bond?"

The jailer reluctantly answered yes. Ralph rushed to his church office a few blocks away to call someone who could produce the cash.

Meanwhile a number of people had assembled in front of the jail. Deacons and trustees of my church were coming from every side. Soon the crowd had become so large that the jailer began to panic. Rushing into the fingerprinting room he said: "King, you can go now," and before I could half get my coat on, he was ushering me out, released on my own bond. He returned my possessions and informed me that my trial would be held on Monday morning at eight-thirty.

As I walked out the front door and noticed the host of friends and well-wishers, I regained the courage that I had temporarily lost. I knew that I did not stand alone. After a brief statement to the crowd, I was driven home by one of my deacons. My wife greeted me with a kiss as I walked in the door. Inside, many members of my church and other friends were waiting anxiously to hear the outcome. Their words of encouragement gave me further assurance that I was not alone.

From that night on my commitment to the struggle for freedom was stronger than ever before. Before retiring I talked with Coretta, and, as usual, she gave me the reassurance that can only come from one who is as close to you as your own heartbeat. Yes, the night of injustice was dark: the "get-tough" policy was taking its toll. But in the darkness I could see a radiant star of unity.

VIII

The Violence of Desperate Men

AFTER the "get-tough" policy failed to stop the movement the diehards became desperate, and we waited to see what their next move would be. Almost immediately after the protest started we had begun to receive threatening telephone calls and letters. Sporadic in the beginning, they increased as time went on. By the middle of January, they had risen to thirty and forty a day.

Postcards, often signed "KKK," said simply "get out of town or else." Many misspelled and crudely written letters presented religious half-truths to prove that "God do not intend the White People and the Negro to go to gather if he did we would be the same." Others enclosed mimeographed and printed materials combining anti-Semitic and anti-Negro sentiments. One of these contained a handwritten postscript: "You niggers are getting your self in a bad place. The Bible is strong for segregation as of the jews concerning other races. It is even for segregation between the 12 tribes of Isareal. We need and will have a Hitler to get our country straightened out." Many of the letters were unprintable catalogues of blasphemy and obscenity.

Meanwhile the telephone rang all day and most of the night. Often Coretta was alone in the house when the calls came, but the insulting voices did not spare her. Many times the person on the other end simply waited until we answered and then hung up.

A large percentage of the calls had sexual themes. One woman, whose voice I soon came to recognize, telephoned day after day to hurl her sexual accusations at the Negro. Whenever I tried to answer, as I frequently did in an effort to explain our case calmly, the caller would cut me off. Occasionally, we would leave the telephone off the hook, but we could not do this for long because we never knew when an important call would come in.

When these incidents started, I took them in stride, feeling that they were the work of a few hotheads who would soon be discouraged when they discovered that we would not fight back. But as the weeks passed, I began to see that many of the threats were in earnest. Soon I felt myself faltering and growing in fear. One day, a white friend told me that he had heard from reliable sources that plans were being made to take my life. For the first time I realized that something could happen to me.

One night at a mass meeting, I found myself saying: "If one day you find me sprawled out dead, I do not want you to retaliate with a single act of violence. I urge you to continue protesting with the same dignity and discipline you have shown so far." A strange silence came over the audience.

Afterward, to the anxious group that gathered around, I tried to make light of the incident by saying that my words had not grown from any specific cause, but were just a general statement of principle that should guide our actions in the event of any fatality. But Ralph Abernathy was not satisfied. As he drove me home that night, he said:

"Something is wrong. You are disturbed about something."

I tried to evade the issue by repeating what I had just told the group at the church. But he persisted.

"Martin," he said, "you were not talking about some general principle. You had something specific in mind."

Unable to evade any longer, I admitted the truth. For the first time I told him about the threats that were harassing my family. I told him about the conversation with my white friend. I told him about the fears that were creeping up on my soul. Ralph tried to reassure me, but I was still afraid.

The threats continued. Almost every day someone warned me that he had overheard white men making plans to get rid of me. Almost every night I went to bed faced with the uncertainty of the next moment. In the morning I would look at Coretta and "Yoki" and say to myself: "They can be taken away from me at any moment; I can be taken away from them at any moment." For once I did not even share my thoughts with Coretta.

One night toward the end of January I settled into bed late, after a strenuous day. Coretta had already fallen asleep and just as I was about to doze off the telephone rang. An angry voice said, "Listen, nigger, we've taken all we want from you; before next week you'll be sorry you ever came to Montgomery." I hung up, but I couldn't sleep. It seemed that all of my fears had come down on me at once. I had reached the saturation point.

I got out of bed and began to walk the floor. Finally I went to the kitchen and heated a pot of coffee. I was ready to give up. With my cup of coffee sitting untouched before me I tried to think of a way to move out of the picture without appearing a coward. In this state of exhaustion, when my courage had all but gone, I decided to take my problem to God. With my head in my hands, I bowed over the kitchen table and prayed aloud. The words I spoke to God that midnight are still vivid in my memory. "I am here taking a stand for what I believe is right. But now I am afraid. The people are looking to me for leadership, and if I stand before them without strength and courage, they too will falter. I am at the end of my powers. I have nothing left. I've come to the point where I can't face it alone."

At that moment I experienced the presence of the Divine as I had never experienced Him before. It seemed as though I could hear the quiet assurance of an inner voice saying: "Stand up for righteousness, stand up for truth; and God will be at your side forever." Almost at once my fears began to go. My uncertainty disappeared. I was ready to face anything.

Three nights later, on January 30, I left home a little before seven to attend our Monday evening mass meeting at the First Baptist Church. A member of my congregation, Mrs. Mary Lucy Williams, had come to the parsonage to keep my wife company in my absence. After putting the baby to bed, Coretta and Mrs. Williams went to the living room to look at television. About nine-thirty they heard a noise in front that sounded as though someone had thrown a brick. In a matter of seconds an explosion rocked the house. A bomb had gone off on the porch.

The sound was heard many blocks away, and word of the bombing reached the mass meeting almost instantly. Toward the close of the meeting, as I stood on the platform helping to take the collection, I noticed an usher rushing to give Ralph Abernathy a message. Abernathy turned and ran downstairs, soon to reappear with a worried look on his face. Several others rushed in and out of the church. People looked at me and then away; one or two seemed about to approach me and then changed their minds. An usher called me to the side of the platform, presumably to give me a message, but before I could get there S. S. Seay had sent him away. By now I was convinced that whatever had happened affected me. I called Ralph Abernathy, S. S. Seay, and E. N. French and asked them to tell me what was wrong. Ralph looked at Seay and French and then turned to me and said hesitantly:

"Your house has been bombed."

I asked if my wife and baby were all right.

They said, "We are checking on that now."

Strangely enough, I accepted the word of the bombing calmly. My religious experience a few nights before had given me the strength to face it. I interrupted the collection and asked all present to give me their undivided attention. After telling them why I had to leave, I urged each person to go straight home after the meeting and adhere strictly to our philosophy of nonviolence. I admonished them not to become panicky and lose their heads. "Let us keep moving," I urged them, "with the faith that what we are doing is right, and with the even greater faith that God is with us in the struggle."

I was immediately driven home. As we neared the scene I noticed hundreds of people with angry faces in front of the house. The policemen were trying, in their usual rough manner, to clear the streets, but they were ignored by the crowd. One Negro was saying to a policeman, who was attempting to push him aside: "I ain't gonna move nowhere. That's the trouble now; you white folks is always pushin' us around. Now you got your .38 and I got mine; so let's battle it out." As I walked toward the front porch I realized that many people were armed. Nonviolent resistance was on the verge of being transformed into violence.

I rushed into the house to see if Coretta and "Yoki" were safe. When I walked into the bedroom and saw my wife and daughter uninjured, I drew my first full breath in many minutes. I learned that fortunately when Coretta and Mrs. Williams had heard the sound of something falling on the front porch, they had jumped up and run to the back of the house. If instead they had gone to the porch to investigate, the outcome might have been fatal. Coretta was neither bitter nor panicky. She had accepted the whole thing with unbelievable composure. As I noticed her calmness I became even more calm myself.

Mayor Gayle, Commissioner Sellers, and several white reporters had reached the house before I did and were standing in the dining room. After reassuring myself about my family's safety, I went to speak to them. Both Gayle and Sellers expressed their regret that "this unfortunate incident has taken place in our city." One of the trustees of my church, who is employed in the public school system of Montgomery, was standing beside me when the mayor and the commissioner spoke. Although in a vulnerable position, he turned to the mayor and said: "You may express your regrets, but you must face the fact that your public statements created the atmosphere for this bombing. This is the end result of your 'get-tough' policy." Neither Mayor Gayle nor Commissioner Sellers could reply.

By this time the crowd outside was getting out of hand. The policemen had failed to disperse them, and throngs of additional people were arriving every minute. The white reporters inside the house wanted to leave to get their stories on the wires, but they were afraid to face the angry crowd. The mayor and police commissioner, though they might not have admitted it, were very pale.

In this atmosphere I walked out to the porch and asked the crowd to come to order. In less than a moment there was complete silence. Quietly I told them that I was all right and that my wife and baby were all right. "Now let's not become panicky," I continued. "If you have weapons, take them home; if you do not have them, please do not seek to get them. We cannot solve this problem through retaliatory violence. We must meet violence with nonviolence. Remember the words of Jesus: 'He who lives by the sword will perish by the sword.'" I then urged them to leave peacefully. "We must love our white brothers," I said, "no matter what they do to us. We must make them know that we love them. Jesus still cries out in words that echo across the centuries: 'Love your enemies; bless them that curse you; pray for them that despitefully use you.' This is what we must live by. We must meet hate with love. Remember," I ended, "if I am stopped, this movement will not stop, because God is with the movement. Go home with this glowing faith and this radiant assurance."

As I finished speaking there were shouts of "Amen" and "God bless you." I could hear voices saying: "We are with you all the way, Reverend." I looked out over that vast throng of people and noticed tears on many faces.

After I finished, the police commissioner began to address the crowd. Immediately there were boos. Police officers tried to get the attention of the Negroes by saying, "Be quiet—the commissioner is speaking." To this the crowd responded with even louder boos. I came back to the edge of the porch and raised my hand for silence. "Remember what I just said. Let us hear the commissioner." In the ensuing lull, the commissioner spoke and offered a reward to the person or persons who could report the offenders. Then the crowd began to disperse.

Things remained tense the whole of that night. The Negroes had had enough. They were ready to meet violence with violence. One policeman later told me that if a Negro had fallen over a brick that night a race riot would probably have broken out because the Negro would have been convinced that a white person had pushed him. This could well have been the darkest night in Montgomery's history. But something happened to avert it: The spirit of God was in our hearts; and a night that seemed destined to end in unleashed chaos came to a close in a majestic group demonstration of nonviolence.

After our many friends left the house late that evening, Coretta, "Yoki," and I were driven to the home of one of our church members to spend the night. I could not get to sleep. While I lay in that quiet front bedroom, with a distant street lamp throwing a reassuring glow through the curtained window, I began to think of the viciousness of people who would bomb my home. I could feel the anger rising when I realized that my wife and baby could have been killed. I thought about the city commissioners and all the statements that they had made about me and the Negro generally. I was once more on the verge of corroding hatred. And once more I caught myself and said: "You must not allow yourself to become bitter."

I tried to put myself in the place of the three commissioners. I said to myself these men are not bad men. They are misguided. They have fine reputations in the community. In their dealings with white people they are respectable and gentlemanly. They probably think they are right in their methods of dealing with Negroes. They say the things they say about us and treat us as they do because they have been taught these things. From the cradle to the grave, it is instilled in them that the Negro is inferior. Their parents probably taught them that; the schools they attended taught them that; the books they read, even their churches and ministers, often taught them that; and above all the very concept of segregation teaches them that. The whole cultural tradition under which they have grown—a tradition blighted with more than 250 years of slavery and more than 90 years of segregation—teaches them that Negroes do not deserve certain things. So these men are merely the children of their culture. When they seek to preserve segregation they are seeking to preserve only what their local folkways have taught them was right.

Midnight had long since passed. Coretta and the baby were sound asleep. It was time for me too to get some rest. At about two-thirty I turned over in bed and fell into a dazed slumber. But the night was not yet over. Some time later Coretta and I were awakened by a slow, steady knocking at the front door. We looked at each other wordlessly in the dim light, and listened as the knocking began again. Through the window we could see the dark outline of a figure on the front porch. Our hosts were sound asleep in the back of the house, and we lay in the front, frozen into inaction. Eventually the sounds stopped and we saw a shadowy figure move across the porch and start down the steps to the street. I pulled myself out of bed, peered through the curtains, and recognized the stocky, reassuring back of Coretta's father.

Obie Scott had heard the news of the bombing over the radio in Marion, and had driven to Montgomery to take Coretta and "Yoki" home with him, "until this thing cools off." We talked together for some time, but although Coretta listened respectfully to her father's persuasions, she would not leave. "I'm sorry, Dad," she said, "but I belong here with Martin." And so Obie Scott drove back to Marion alone.

Just two nights later, a stick of dynamite was thrown on the lawn of E. D. Nixon. Fortunately, again no one was hurt. Once more a large crowd of Negroes assembled, but they did not lose control. And so nonviolence had won its first and its second tests.

After the bombings, many of the officers of my church and other trusted friends urged me to hire a bodyguard and armed watchmen for my house. I tried to tell them that I had no fears now, and consequently needed no protection. But they were insistent, so I agreed to consider the question. I also went down to the sheriff's office and applied for a license to carry a gun in the car; but this was refused.

Meanwhile I reconsidered. How could I serve as one of the leaders of a nonviolent movement and at the same time use weapons of violence for my personal protection? Coretta and I talked the matter over for several days and finally agreed that arms were no solution. We decided then to get rid of the one weapon we owned. We tried to satisfy our friends by having floodlights mounted around the house, and hiring unarmed watchmen around the clock. I also promised that I would not travel around the city alone.

This was a comparatively easy promise to keep, thanks to our friend, Bob Williams, professor of music at Alabama State College and a former collegemate of mine at Morehouse. When I came to Montgomery, I had found him here, and from the moment the protest started he was seldom far from my side or Coretta's. He did most of my driving around Montgomery and accompanied me on several out-of-town trips. Whenever Coretta and "Yoki" went to Atlanta or Marion, he was always there to drive them down and to bring them back. Almost imperceptibly he had become my voluntary "bodyguard," though he carried no arms and could never have been as fierce as the name implied.

In this crisis the officers and members of my church were always nearby to lend their encouragement and active support. As I gradually lost my role as husband and father, having to be away from home for hours and sometimes days at a time, the women of the church came into the house to keep Coretta company. Often they volunteered to cook the meals and clean, or help with the baby. Many of the men took turns as watchmen, or drove me around when Bob Williams was not available. Nor did my congregation ever complain when the multiplicity of my new responsibilities caused me to lag in my pastoral duties. For months my day-to-day contact with my parishioners had almost ceased. I had become no more than a Sunday preacher. But my church willingly shared me with the community, and threw their own considerable resources of time and money into the struggle.

Our local white friends, too, came forward with their support. Often they called Coretta to say an encouraging word, and when the house was bombed several of them, known and unknown to us, came by to express their regret. Occasionally the mail would bring a letter from a white Montgomerian saying, "Carry on, we are with you a hundred per cent." Frequently these were simply signed "a white friend."

Interestingly enough, for some time after the bombings the threatening telephone calls slowed up. But this was only a lull; several months later they had begun again in full force. In order to sleep at night, it finally became necessary to apply for an unlisted number. This number was passed out to all the members of the church, the members of the MIA, and other friends across the country. And although it had sometimes been suggested that our own group was responsible for the threats, we never received another hostile call. Of course, the letters still came, but my secretaries were discreet enough to keep as many of them as possible from my attention.

When the opposition discovered that violence could not block the protest, they resorted to mass arrests. As early as January 9, a Montgomery attorney had called the attention of the press to an old state law against boycotts. He referred to Title 14, Section 54, which provides that when two or more persons enter into a conspiracy to prevent the operation of a lawful business, without just cause or legal excuse, they shall be guilty of a misdemeanor. On February 13 the Montgomery County Grand Jury was called to determine whether Negroes who were boycotting the buses were violating this law. After about a week of deliberations, the jury, composed of seventeen whites and one Negro, found the boycott illegal and indicted more than one hundred persons. My name, of course, was on the list.

At the time of the indictments I was at Fisk University in Nashville, giving a series of lectures. During this period I was talking to Montgomery on the phone at least three times a day in order to keep abreast of developments. Thus I heard of the indictments first in a telephone call from Ralph Abernathy, late Tuesday night, February 21. He said that the arrests were scheduled to begin the following morning. Knowing that he would be one of the first to be arrested, I assured him that I would be with him and the others in my prayers. As usual he was unperturbed. I told him that I would cut my trip short in Nashville and come to Montgomery the next day.

I booked an early morning flight. All night long I thought of the people in Montgomery. Would these mass arrests so frighten them that they would urge us to call off the protest? I knew how hard-pressed they had been. For more than thirteen weeks they had walked, and sacrificed, and worn down their cars. They had been harassed and intimidated on every hand. And now they faced arrest on top of all this. Would they become battle-weary, I wondered. Would they give up in despair? Would this be the end of our movement?

I arose early Wednesday morning, and notified the officials of Fisk that I had to leave ahead of time because of the situation in Montgomery. I flew to Atlanta to pick up my wife and daughter, whom I had left at my parents' home while I was in Nashville. My wife, my mother and father met me at the airport. I had told them about the indictments over the phone, and they had gotten additional information from a radio broadcast. Coretta showed her usual composure; but my parents' faces wore signs of deep perturbation.

My father, so unafraid for himself, had fallen into a constant state of terror for me and my family. Since the protest began he had beaten a path between Atlanta and Montgomery to be at our side. Many times he had sat in on our board meetings and never

shown any doubt about the justice of our actions. Yet this stern
and courageous man had reached the point where he could
scarcely mention the protest without tears. My mother too had
suffered. After the bombing she had had to take to bed under
doctor's orders, and she was often ill later. Their expressions—
even the way they walked, I realized as they came toward me at
the airport—had begun to show the strain.

As we drove to their house, my father said that he thought it
would be unwise for me to return to Montgomery now. "Although many others have been indicted," he said, "their main
concern is to get you. They might even put you in jail without a
bond." He went on to tell me that the law enforcement agencies
in Montgomery had been trying to find something on my record in
Atlanta which would make it possible to deport me from Alabama. They had gone to the Atlanta police department, and were
disappointed when Chief Jenkins informed them that I did not
have even a minor police record. "All of this shows," my father
concluded, "that they are out to get you."

I listened to him attentively, and yet I knew that I could not
follow his suggestion and stay in Atlanta. I was profoundly concerned about my parents. I was worried about their worry. I knew
that if I continued the struggle I would be plagued by the pain
that I was inflicting on them. But if I eased out now I would be
plagued by my own conscience, reminding me that I lacked the
moral courage to stand by a cause to the end. No one can understand my conflict who has not looked into the eyes of those he
loves, knowing that he has no alternative but to take a dangerous
stand that leaves them tormented.

My father told me that he had asked several trusted friends
to come to the house in the early afternoon to discuss the whole
issue. Feeling that this exchange of ideas might help to relieve
his worries, I readily agreed to stay over and talk to them. Among

those who came were A. T. Walden, a distinguished attorney; C. R. Yates and T. M. Alexander, both prominent businessmen; C. A. Scott, editor of *Atlanta Daily World*; Bishop Sherman L. Green of A. M. E. Church; Benjamin E. Mays, president of Morehouse College; and Rufus E. Clement, president of Atlanta University. Coretta and my mother joined us.

My father explained to the group that because of his respect for their judgment he was calling on them for advice on whether I should return to Montgomery. He gave them a brief history of the attempts that had been made to get me out of Montgomery. He admitted that the fear of what might happen to me had caused him and my mother many restless nights. He concluded by saying that he had talked to a liberal white attorney a few hours earlier, who had confirmed his feeling that I should not go back at this time.

There were murmurs of agreement in the room, and I listened as sympathetically and objectively as I could while two of the men gave their reasons for concurring. These were my elders, leaders among my people. Their words commanded respect. But soon I could not restrain myself any longer. "I must go back to Montgomery," I protested. "My friends and associates are being arrested. It would be the height of cowardice for me to stay away. I would rather be in jail ten years than desert my people now. I have begun the struggle, and I can't turn back. I have reached the point of no return." In the moment of silence that followed I heard my father break into tears. I looked at Dr. Mays, one of the great influences in my life. Perhaps he heard my unspoken plea. At any rate, he was soon defending my position strongly. Then others joined him in supporting me. They assured my father that things were not so bad as they seemed. Mr. Walden put through two calls on the spot to Thurgood Marshall, general counsel of the NAACP, and Arthur Shores, NAACP counsel in Alabama, both of whom assured him that I would have the best legal protection. In the face of all of these persuasions, my father began to be reconciled to my return to Montgomery.

After everybody had gone, Coretta and I went upstairs to our room and had a long talk. She, too, I was glad to find, had no doubt that I must go back immediately. With my own feelings reinforced by the opinions of others I trusted, and with my father's misgivings at rest, I felt better and more prepared to face the experience ahead.

Characteristically, my father, having withdrawn his objections to our return to Montgomery, decided to go along with us, unconcerned with any possible danger or unpleasantness to himself. He secured a driver and at six o'clock Thursday morning we were on the highway headed for Montgomery, arriving about nine. Before we could get out of the car, several television cameras were trained on us. The reporters had somehow discovered the time of our arrival. A few minutes later Ralph Abernathy, released on bail after his arrest the previous day, came to the house. With Ralph and my father, I set out for the county jail, several of my church members following after.

At the jail, an almost holiday atmosphere prevailed. On the way Ralph Abernathy told me how people had rushed down to get arrested the day before. No one, it seems, had been frightened. No one had tried to evade arrest. Many Negroes had gone voluntarily to the sheriff's office to see if their names were on the list, and were even disappointed when they were not. A once fear-ridden people had been transformed. Those who had previously trembled before the law were now proud to be arrested for the cause of freedom. With this feeling of solidarity around me, I walked with firm steps toward the rear of the jail. After I had received a number and had been photographed and fingerprinted, one of my church members paid my bond and I left for home.

The trial was set for March 19. Friends from all over the country came to Montgomery to be with us during the proceedings. Ministers from as far north as New York were present. Negro Congressman Charles C. Diggs (D-Mich.) was on hand. Scores of reporters representing publications in the United States, India, France, and England were there to cover the trial. More than five hundred Negroes stood in the halls and the streets surrounding the small courthouse. Several of them wore crosses on their lapels reading, "Father, forgive them."

Judge Eugene Carter brought the court to order, and after the necessary preliminaries the state called me up as the first defendant. For four days I sat in court listening to arguments and waiting for a verdict. William F. Thetford, solicitor for the state, was attempting to prove that I had disobeyed a law by organizing an illegal boycott. The defense attorneys—Arthur Shores, Peter Hall, Ozell Billingsley, Fred Gray, Charles Langford, and Robert Carter—presented arguments to show that the prosecution's evidence was insufficient to prove that I had violated Alabama's anti-boycott law. Even if the state had proved such action, they asserted, no evidence was produced to show that the Negroes did not have just cause or legal excuse.

In all, twenty-eight witnesses were brought to the stand by the defense. I listened with a mixture of sadness and awe as these simple people—most of them unlettered—sat on the witness stand without fear and told their stories. They looked the solicitor and the judge in the eye with a courage and dignity to which there was no answer.

Perhaps the most touching testimony was that of Mrs. Stella Brooks. Her husband had climbed on a bus. After paying his fare he was ordered by the driver to get off and reboard by the back door. He looked through the crowded bus and seeing that there was no room in back he said that he would get off and walk if the driver would return his dime. The driver refused; an argument ensued; and the driver called the police. The policeman arrived, abusing Brooks, who still refused to leave the bus unless his dime was returned. The policeman shot him. It happened so suddenly that everybody was dazed. Brooks died of his wounds.

Mrs. Martha Walker testified about the day when she was leading her blind husband from the bus. She had stepped down and as her husband was following the driver slammed the door and began to drive off. Walker's leg was caught. Although Mrs. Walker called out, the driver failed to stop, and her husband was dragged some distance before he could free himself. She reported the incident, but the bus company did nothing about it.

The stories continued. Mrs. Sadie Brooks testified that she heard a Negro passenger threatened because he did not have the correct change. "The driver whipped out a pistol and drove the man off the bus." Mrs. Della Perkins described being called an "ugly black ape" by a driver.

I will always remember my delight when Mrs. Georgia Gilmore —an unlettered woman of unusual intelligence—told how an operator demanded that she get off the bus after paying her fare and board it again by the back door, and then drove away before she could get there. She turned to Judge Carter and said: "When they count the money, they do not know Negro money from white money."

On Thursday afternoon, March 22, both sides rested. All eyes were turned toward Judge Carter, as with barely a pause he rendered his verdict: "I declare the defendant guilty of violating the state's anti-boycott law." The penalty was a fine of $500 and court costs, or 386 days at hard labor in the County of Montgomery. Then Judge Carter announced that he was giving a minimum penalty because of what I had done to prevent violence. In the cases of the other Negroes charged with the same violation—the number had now boiled down to 89—Judge Carter entered a continuance until a final appeal was complete in my case.

In a few minutes several friends had come up to sign my bond, and the lawyers had notified the judge that the case would be appealed. Many people stood around the courtroom in tears. Others walked out with their heads bowed. I came to the end of my trial with a feeling of sympathy for Judge Carter in his dilemma. To convict me he had to face the condemnation of the nation and world opinion; to acquit me he had to face the condemnation of the local community and those voters who kept him in office. Throughout the proceedings he had treated me with great courtesy, and he had rendered a verdict which he probably thought was the best way out. After the trial he left town for a "welcomed rest."

I left the courtroom with my wife at my side and a host of friends following. In front of the courthouse hundreds of Negroes and whites, including television cameramen and photographers, were waiting. As I waved my hand, they shouted: "God bless you," and began to sing, "We ain't gonna ride the buses no more."

Ordinarily, a person leaving a courtroom with a conviction behind him would wear a somber face. But I left with a smile. I knew that I was a convicted criminal, but I was proud of my crime. It was the crime of joining my people in a nonviolent protest against injustice. It was the crime of seeking to instill within my people a sense of dignity and self-respect. It was the crime of desiring for my people the unalienable rights of life, liberty, and the pursuit of happiness. It was above all the crime of seeking to convince my people that noncoöperation with evil is just as much a moral duty as is coöperation with good.

So ended another effort to halt the protest. Instead of stopping the movement, the opposition's tactics had only served to give it greater momentum, and to draw us closer together. What the opposition failed to see was that our mutual sufferings had wrapped us all in a single garment of destiny. What happened to one happened to all.

On that cloudy afternoon in March, Judge Carter had convicted more than Martin Luther King, Jr., Case No. 7399; he had convicted every Negro in Montgomery. It is no wonder that the movement couldn't be stopped. It was too large to be stopped. Its links were too well bound together in a powerfully effective chain. There is amazing power in unity. Where there is true unity, every effort to disunite only serves to strengthen the unity This is what the opposition failed to see.

The members of the opposition had also revealed that they did not know the Negroes with whom they were dealing. They thought they were dealing with a group who could be cajoled or forced to do whatever the white man wanted them to do. They were not aware that they were dealing with Negroes who had been freed from fear. And so every move they made proved to be a mistake. It could not be otherwise, because their methods were geared to the "old Negro," and they were dealing with a "new Negro."

IX

Desegregation at Last

FROM the beginning of the bus protest most
of the Negro leaders lived with the hope that a settlement would
soon be worked out. Our demands were limited, moderate enough
to permit adjustment within the segregation laws. Even the most
conservative white person could go along with them, we reasoned. But as the days and months unfolded we discovered that
our optimism was misplaced. The intransigence of the city commission, the crudeness of the "get-tough" policy, and the viciousness of the recent bombings convinced us all that an attack must
be made upon bus segregation itself. Accordingly a suit was filed
in the United States Federal District Court, asking for an end
of bus segregation on the grounds that it was contrary to the
Fourteenth Amendment. The court was also asked to stop the city
commissioners from violating the civil rights of Negro motorists
and pedestrians.

The hearing was set for May 11, 1956, before a three-judge
federal court panel. It was a great relief to be in a federal court.
Here the atmosphere of justice prevailed. No one can understand the feeling that comes to a Southern Negro on entering
a federal court unless he sees with his own eyes and feels with
his own soul the tragic sabotage of justice in the city and state
courts of the South. The Negro goes into these courts knowing
that the cards are stacked against him. Here he is virtually certain

151

to face a prejudiced jury or a biased judge, and is openly robbed with little hope of redress. But the Southern Negro goes into the federal court with the feeling that he has an honest chance of justice before the law.

Our suit was filed by the same attorneys who had acted for the defense before Judge Carter in the boycott case. This time they presented persuasive arguments against the constitutionality of segregation itself. Robert Carter of the legal staff of the NAACP argued against the validity of the old Plessy Doctrine. This doctrine, first promulgated by the United States Supreme Court in 1896, had given legal validity to the Southern institution of separate-but-equal facilities for Negroes and whites. In the area of education, the Supreme Court had already reversed this position in its historic decision of May 1954; but the Plessy Doctrine still remained as the rationale of segregation in other areas. This injustice and inconsistency in the segregation laws was the object of Bob Carter's brilliant attack. Meanwhile the city attorneys, throughout their argument, dwelt on a single theme: if bus segregation ended, Montgomery would become a battleground of violence and bloodshed.

After listening to these arguments for several hours, Judge Rives addressed the city attorneys. "Is it fair," he asked, "to command one man to surrender his constitutional rights, if they are his constitutional rights, in order to prevent another man from committing a crime?" At this I touched Ralph Abernathy, who was sitting on one side of me, and Vernon Johns (he was on a brief visit to Montgomery at this time), on the other side, and whispered: "It looks as though we might get a favorable verdict."

The judges deliberated for about three weeks. On June 4, 1956, they declared in a two-to-one decision, Judge Lynn of Birmingham dissenting, that the city bus segregation laws of Alabama were unconstitutional. The city attorneys immediately announced that they would appeal the case to the United States Supreme Court.

The battle was not yet won. We would have to walk and sacrifice for several more months, while the city appealed the case. But at least we could walk with new hope. Now it was only a matter of time.

Or so we thought. But almost on the heels of the court's decision, disaster threatened the movement from a new quarter. On June 11, Rev. U. J. Fields made a statement to the press claiming that he was resigning as recording secretary of the MIA. In his announcement the youthful, goateed pastor of the Bell Street Baptist Church, who had been an officer of the Association from the beginning, accused the members of "misusing money sent from all over the nation," and appropriating it "for their own purposes." Many of the leaders, he claimed, had taken on an air of "bigness" and had become "too egotistical and interested in perpetuating themselves." The Association, he said, no longer represented what he had stood for, and he was severing his relations with a movement in which "the many are exploited by the few."

I was out of the city when Fields released his statement. Coretta and I had driven to California with Ralph and Juanita Abernathy to attend some conferences, and to enjoy our first vacation together away from the daily tensions of the protest. Rev. R. J. Glasco, then administrative assistant at the MIA office, telephoned the news. Earlier in the evening Fields had come to the mass meeting indignant because the executive board had failed to re-elect him to office. When he brought the matter before the audience, he was further enraged by their almost unanimous approval of the board's action. He had left the meeting immediately to announce his "resignation" and prepare his attack on the MIA.

Although the news did not come entirely as a surprise, I realized the seriousness of the possible repercussions. While I was certain that there was no truth in Fields's charges, I knew that some people would believe them, and that many others would be left in a state of confusion. A charge of misappropriation of funds could cause a curtailment of contributions, thus hampering the car pool. Moreover, the white opposition would welcome this break as an opportunity to investigate our books with the ultimate aim of freezing our funds. I was also worried about how the Negroes of Montgomery might express their resentment against Fields.

My vacation had ended before it had well begun. I canceled the remainder of my engagements, promising to rejoin Coretta and the Abernathys later, and flew back to Montgomery. There I found, as I had expected, that emotions were running high. No one would speak in Fields's support, and so obviously distorted were his charges that even the local white press reported them with little enthusiasm. The Negroes were describing him as either a "fool" or a "black Judas." "I jest wish I could get my hands on him," said one indignant maid. The group of his own congregation had met and voted him out. (He was subsequently reinstated.) Everywhere in the Negro community sentiment mounted against him.

Fortunately by this time Fields had privately confessed to several people that he deeply regretted what he had done. Early on the morning of June 18 my telephone rang. Fields had learned that I was back in town, and wanted to see me. He arrived with a sober face, and went immediately to the point.

"I want you to know that I was not referring to you in my accusations. I have always had the greatest respect for your integrity and I still do. But there are some members of the MIA board that I don't care for at all. We never could get along."

I interrupted him. "You mean that your statements about the

egotism of the leaders grew out of a personal conflict between you and one or two men on the board?"

"Yes," he admitted, "I guess that is true."

I asked him about the charge of misappropriation of funds, saying that if any such thing existed I wanted to know about it. With chagrin Fields answered:

"I confess that I don't know a single instance of misappropriation. All of those things I made up in a moment of anger. I felt that I had been mistreated by the board, and this was my way of retaliating."

By now it was clear that Fields was more to be pitied than scorned. I asked if he would be willing to make the same statements in the mass meeting that night. With some apprehension, he agreed.

People started assembling in front of the Beulah Baptist Church at three that afternoon. By five the church was filled. In the sweltering evening there was an unaccustomed atmosphere of bitterness. When Fields joined me on the rostrum at seven, the crowd muttered angrily, and I heard one voice call out, "Look at that devil sitting right next to Reverend King."

I had a double task ahead: one was to convince the people that there had been no misappropriation of funds and that the internal structure of the MIA was still stable; the other was to persuade them to forgive Fields for his errors and to give him a hearing. I plunged immediately into the first issue.

"I guess," I said, "that I know as much about the MIA as anyone in Montgomery, and I can truthfully say that I do not know of a single instance of misappropriation of funds. The finance committee of our Association is composed of honest men and women—persons whose integrity has been established over the years and whose character is above reproach. I have implicit faith in the finance committee and the ministers who have spoken at fund-raising meetings all over the country."

I denied the accusation of "bigness." "It is true," I said, "that some of the leaders have received national and international publicity, but only the shallow-minded are excited over publicity. Publicity is evanescent; it is here today and gone tomorrow. Today Autherine Lucy is showered with publicity; tomorrow it is Gus Courts. Today it is Emmet Till, tomorrow it is Martin Luther King. Then in another tomorrow it will be somebody else. Whoever falls in love with publicity is not fit to have it and will end up in misery.

"The honors and privileges," I continued, "that often come as a result of leadership constitute only one side of the picture. The greater the privileges, the greater the responsibilities and sacrifices."

So far the audience had listened sympathetically. But when I began to speak about Fields, they moved restlessly in their seats and I could hear a low murmur of disapproval. I expressed frank regret at Fields's statement. "Certainly it has created many unnecessary problems for us."

"You said it, Reverend," someone shouted.

"But," I continued, "we must meet this situation with the same dignity and discipline with which we have met so many difficult situations in the past. Let us never forget that we have committed ourselves to a way of nonviolence, and nonviolence means avoiding not only external physical violence but also internal violence of spirit. You not only refuse to shoot a man, but you refuse to hate him. Now in the spirit of our nonviolent movement I call upon you to forgive the Reverend Fields." I could see a few heads shaking in refusal, but I did not stop speaking. "We are all aware of the weaknesses of human nature. We have all made mistakes along the way of life, and we have all had moments when our emotions overpowered us. Now some of us are here this evening to stone one of our brothers because he has made a mistake." I paused a moment, and then spoke the words of Christ: "Let him who is without sin cast the first stone." With this a deep hush came across the audience.

In conclusion I recited the parable of the prodigal son. "Will we be like the unforgiving elder brother, or will we, in the spirit of Christ, follow the example of the loving and forgiving father?"

As Fields rose to speak, instead of the boos and catcalls he had expected he was met with respectful silence. He began to pray. "Lord, help us to live in such a way from day to day, that even when we kneel to pray, our prayers will be for others. . . ." A great amen came from the audience. Then he asked forgiveness for his mistake, and assured the group that he had no evidence that money had been misused or misplaced by the MIA. By the time he had finished the group was deeply moved. He left the platform to solid applause.

So nonviolence triumphed again, and a situation that many had predicted would be the end of the MIA left it more united than ever in the spirit of tolerance.

The summer days gave way to the shorter cooler days of an Alabama autumn. The Supreme Court decision on our appeal was still pending. Meanwhile we were facing continued attempts to block the car pool. Insurance agents decided, almost overnight, to refuse to insure our station wagons, contending that the risk was too high. The liability insurance on our station wagons was canceled no less than four times within four months. (We had no trouble with the collision insurance because it was with a Negro company.)

Finally the company that held our liability insurance notified us that all the policies would be canceled as of September 15. A Northern friend who had read of our trouble wrote suggesting that we contact Lloyds of London. A few days later I talked to T. M. Alexander, an insurance broker in Atlanta, who approved of the idea and agreed to make the contact for us. In a few days he was able to tell us that Lloyds of London would take the insurance. From that moment on our insurance problems were solved.

But we were in for even greater difficulties. The city decided to take legal action against the car pool itself. On October 30, 1956, Mayor Gayle introduced a resolution instructing the city's legal department "to file such proceedings as it may deem proper to stop the operation of car pool or transportation systems growing out of the bus boycott." We tried to block this maneuver by filing a request in the federal court for an order restraining the city from interfering with the pool. But U. S. District Judge Frank M. Johnson refused to grant the request. Soon several of us received subpoenas; the city had filed the petition. The hearing was set for Tuesday, November 13.

The night before the hearing I had to go before the mass meeting to warn the people that the car pool would probably be enjoined. I knew that they had willingly suffered for nearly twelve months, but how could they function at all with the car pool destroyed? Could we ask them to walk back and forth every day to their jobs? And if not, would we then be forced to admit that the protest had failed in the end? For the first time in our long struggle together, I almost shrank from appearing before them.

The evening came, and I mustered up enough courage to tell them the truth. I tried, however, to end on a note of hope. "This may well be," I said, "the darkest hour just before dawn. We have moved all of these months with the daring faith that God was with us in our struggle. The many experiences of days gone by have vindicated that faith in a most unexpected manner. We must go out with the same faith, the same conviction. We must believe that a way will be made out of no way." But in spite of these words, I could feel the cold breeze of pessimism passing through the audience. It was a dark night—darker than a thousand midnights. It was a night in which the light of hope was about to fade away and the lamp of faith about to flicker. We went home with nothing before us but a cloud of uncertainty.

Tuesday morning found us in court, once again before Judge Carter. The city's petition was directed against the MIA and several churches and individuals. It asked the court to grant the city compensation for damages growing out of the car pool operation. The city contended that it had lost more than $15,000 as a result of the reduction in bus travel (the city receives 2 per cent of the bus company revenues). It further alleged that the car pool was a "public nuisance" and a "private enterprise" operating without license fee or franchise. As the arguments unfolded the issue boiled down to this: Was the car pool a "private enterprise" operating without a franchise? Or was it a voluntary "share-a-ride" plan provided as a service by Negro churches without a profit?

As chief defendant I sat at the front table with the prosecuting and defense attorneys. Around twelve o'clock—during a brief recess—I noticed unusual commotion in the courtroom. Both Commissioner Sellers and Mayor Gayle were called to a back room, followed by two of the city attorneys. Several reporters moved excitedly in and out of the room.

I turned to Fred Gray and Peter Hall and said: "Something is wrong."

Before I could fully get these words out, Rex Thomas—a reporter for Associated Press—came up to me with a paper in his hand.

"Here is the decision that you have been waiting for. Read this release."

Quickly, with a mixture of anxiety and hope, I read these words: "The United States Supreme Court today affirmed a decision of a special three-judge U. S. District Court in declaring Alabama's state and local laws requiring segregation on buses unconstitutional. The Supreme Court acted without listening to any argument; it simply said 'the motion to affirm is granted and the Judgment is affirmed.'"

At this moment my heart began to throb with an inexpressible joy. The darkest hour of our struggle had indeed proved to be the first hour of victory. At once I told the news to the attorneys at the table. Then I rushed to the back of the room to tell my wife, Ralph Abernathy, and E. D. Nixon. Soon the word had spread to the whole courtroom. The faces of the Negroes showed that they had heard. "God Almighty has spoken from Washington, D.C.," said one joyful bystander.

After a few minutes Judge Carter called the court to order again, and we settled down to the case at hand for the remainder of the day. About five o'clock both sides rested, and the judge's decision came in a matter of minutes: As we had all expected, the city was granted a temporary injunction to halt the motor pool. But the decision was an anticlimax. Tuesday, November 13, 1956, will always remain an important and ironic date in the history of the Montgomery bus protest. On that day two historic decisions were rendered—one to do away with the pool; the other to remove the underlying conditions that made it necessary.

I rushed home and notified the press that I was calling the Negro citizens together on Wednesday night, November 14, to decide whether to call off the protest. In order to accommodate as many people as possible, two simultaneous meetings were scheduled, one on each side of town, with the speakers traveling from one meeting to the other. In the meantime, the executive board decided, on the advice of counsel, to recommend that the official protest be ended immediately, but that the return to the buses be delayed until the mandatory order arrived from the Supreme Court in Washington. It was expected in a few days.

The eight thousand men and women who crowded in and around the two churches were in high spirits. At the first meeting it was clear that the news of the decision had spread fast, and the opening hymn had a special note of joy. Reading the Scripture that night was Bob Graetz, who had chosen Paul's famous letter to the Corinthians: "Though I have all faith, so that I could remove mountains, and have not love, I am nothing. . . . Love suffereth long, and is kind. . . ."

When the slender blond minister came to the words: "When I was a child, I spoke as a child, I understood as a child, I thought as a child: but when I became a man, I put away childish things," the congregation burst into applause. Soon they were shouting and cheering and waving their handkerchiefs, as if to say that they knew they had come of age, had won new dignity. When Bob Graetz concluded: "And now abideth faith, hope, love, but the greatest of these is love," there was another spontaneous outburst. Only a people who had struggled to love in the midst of bitter conflict could have reacted in this fashion. I knew then that nonviolence, for all its difficulties, had won its way into our hearts.

Later Ralph Abernathy spoke. He told how a white newspaperman had reproached him for this outburst on the part of the congregation.

"Isn't it a little peculiar," the journalist had asked, "for people to interrupt the Scripture in that way?"

"Yes it is," Abernathy quoted himself in reply. "Just as it is peculiar for people to walk in the snow and rain when there are empty buses available; just as it is peculiar for people to pray for those who persecute them; just as it is peculiar for the Southern Negro to stand up and look a white man in the face as an equal." At this his audience laughed and shouted and applauded.

Each of the meetings accepted the recommendations of the executive board to call off the protest but refrain from riding the buses until the mandate reached Alabama.

That night the Ku Klux Klan rode. The radio had announced their plan to demonstrate throughout the Negro community, and threats of violence and new bombings were in the air. My mail was warning that "if you allow the niggers to go back on the buses and sit in the front seats we're going to burn down fifty houses in one night, including yours." Another letter cursed the Supreme Court and threatened "that damn Hugo Black": "When he comes back to Alabama we're going to hang you and him from the same tree."

Ordinarily, threats of Klan action were a signal to the Negroes to go into their houses, close the doors, pull the shades, or turn off the lights. Fearing death, they played dead. But this time they had prepared a surprise. When the Klan arrived—according to the newspapers "about forty carloads of robed and hooded members"—porch lights were on and doors open. As the Klan drove by, the Negroes behaved as though they were watching a circus parade. Concealing the effort it cost them, many walked about as usual; some simply watched from their steps; a few waved at the passing cars. After a few blocks, the Klan, nonplused, turned off into a sidestreet and disappeared into the night.

Soon we discovered that it was going to take the mandate more than four or five days to reach Montgomery. A reporter in contact with the clerk of the Court in Washington revealed that it would be closer to a month. This created a serious problem since the car pool was still enjoined. To meet this crisis we suggested that each area and street work out a coöperative "share-a-ride" plan

With S. S. Seay as skillful coördinator, the plan succeeded. The buses remained empty.

Meanwhile we went to work to prepare the people for integrated buses. In mass meeting after mass meeting we stressed nonviolence. The prevailing theme was that "we must not take this as a victory over the white man, but as a victory for justice and democracy." We hammered away at the point that "we must not go back on the buses and push people around unnecessarily boasting of our rights. We must simply sit where there is a vacant seat."

In several meetings we ran teaching sessions to school the people in nonviolent techniques. We lined up chairs in front of the altar to resemble a bus, with a driver's seat out front. From the audience we selected a dozen or so "actors" and assigned each one a role in a hypothetical situation. One man was driver and the others were white and Negro passengers. Both groups contained some hostile and some courteous characters. As the audience watched, the actors played out a scene of insult or violence. At the end of each scene the actors returned to the audience and another group took their place; and at the end of each session a general discussion followed.

Sometimes the person playing a white man put so much zeal into his performance that he had to be gently reproved from the sidelines. Often a Negro forgot his nonviolent role and struck back with vigor; whenever this happened we worked to rechannel his words and deeds in a nonviolent direction.

As the day for the mandate drew near, several MIA leaders went into the schools and urged the high school and college students to adhere to the way of nonviolence. We also distributed throughout the city a mimeographed list of "Suggestions for Integrating Buses." In preparing this text we had the assistance of the Rev. Glenn Smiley, a Southern-born white minister of the Fellowship of Reconciliation who was in Montgomery at the time.

INTEGRATED BUS SUGGESTIONS

This is a historic week because segregation on buses has now been declared unconstitutional. Within a few days the Supreme Court Mandate will reach Montgomery and you will be re-boarding *integrated* buses. This places upon us all a tremendous responsibility of maintaining, in face of what could be some unpleasantness, a calm and loving dignity befitting good citizens and members of our race. If there is violence in word or deed it must not be our people who commit it.

For your help and convenience the following suggestions are made. Will you read, study and memorize them so that our non-violent determination may not be endangered. First, some general suggestions:

1. Not all white people are opposed to integrated buses. Accept good-will on the part of many.
2. The *whole* bus is now for the use of *all* people. Take a vacant seat.
3. Pray for guidance and commit yourself to complete non-violence in word and action as you enter the bus.
4. Demonstrate the calm dignity of our Montgomery people in your actions.
5. In all things observe ordinary rules of courtesy and good behavior.
6. Remember that this is not a victory for Negroes alone, but for all Montgomery and the South. Do not boast! Do not brag!
7. Be quiet but friendly; proud, but not arrogant; joyous, but not boisterous.
8. Be loving enough to absorb evil and understanding enough to turn an enemy into a friend.

Now for some specific suggestions:

1. The bus driver is in charge of the bus and has been instructed to obey the law. Assume that he will coöperate in helping you occupy any vacant seat.
2. Do not deliberately sit by a white person, unless there is no other seat.
3. In sitting down by a person, white or colored, say "May I" or "Pardon me" as you sit. This is a common courtesy.
4. If cursed, do not curse back. If pushed, do not push back. If struck, do not strike back, but evidence love and goodwill at all times.

STRATEGY

The protest leaders meet often and at all hours. *Above,* left to right: S. S. Seay, H. H. Hubbard, M. L. King, and R. J. Glasco carry on at the end of an Executive Board meeting. *Left:* Rufus Lewis and B. J. Simms discuss transportation committee business.

OPPOSITION

Meanwhile the white community takes steps. *Above:* White Citizens Council in session. *Below:* a motorcycle policeman trails a pool-car.

Above: Ralph Abernathy's house, after the bombers have finished. *Below, left:* Case 7089; *right:* the Associated Press news picture that led to reports of the author's collapse. (See page 178.)

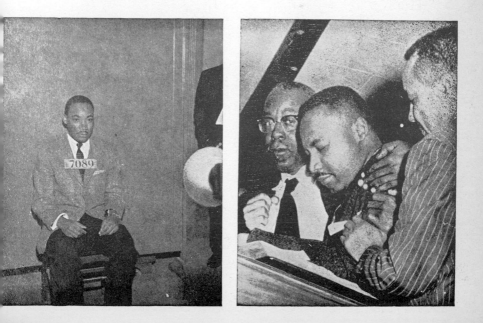

THE END

The first non-segregated bus rides down the streets of Montgomery with Glenn
Smiley, a white Southerner, sharing a seat with M. L. King. Ralph Abernathy (in
front) and two other passengers enjoy the fruits of the year-long struggle. (E. D.
Nixon sat across the aisle.) *Below,* family portrait: Mr. and Mrs. M. L. King, Sr.,
Coretta, and "Yoki."

5. In case of an incident, talk as little as possible, and always in a quiet tone. Do not get up from your seat! Report all serious incidents to the bus driver.

6. For the first few days try to get on the bus with a friend in whose non-violence you have confidence. You can uphold one another by a glance or a prayer.

7. If another person is being molested, do not arise to go to his defense, but pray for the oppressor and use moral and spiritual force to carry on the struggle for justice.

8. According to your own ability and personality, do not be afraid to experiment with new and creative techniques for achieving reconciliation and social change.

9. If you feel you cannot take it, walk for another week or two. We have confidence in our people. GOD BLESS YOU ALL.

In spite of all of our efforts to prepare the Negroes for integrated buses, not a single white group would take the responsibility of preparing the white community. We tried to get the white ministerial alliance to make a simple statement calling for courtesy and Christian brotherhood, but in spite of the favorable response of a few ministers, Robert Graetz reported that the majority "dared not get involved in such a controversial issue." This was a deep disappointment. Although the white ministers as a group had been appallingly silent throughout the protest, I had still maintained the hope that they would take a stand once the decision was rendered. Yes, there were always a few; but they were far too rare.

The only white group that came near to making a positive statement was the Men of Montgomery, the businessmen who had already shown their good will in their earlier efforts to settle the protest. About ten days before the mandate came to Montgomery, a committee of the Men of Montgomery met with a group from the MIA and worked out a statement, calling for courtesy and nonviolence, to be issued jointly. When the statement was presented to the full membership of the Men of Montgomery, however, two or three members objected to it and, since unanimous approval was required, the release of the statement was blocked. Thus passed the one opportunity of the white community to take a positive stand for law and order.

Soon the reactionaries had taken over. A White Citizens Council leader threatened: "Any attempt to enforce this decision will lead to riot and bloodshed." One group suggested the establishment of a fleet of station wagons for a white pick-up service—an interesting proposal from those who had just succeeded in outlawing the Negro fleet! On December 18, the City Commissioners issued the following statement:

> This decision in the bus case has had a tremendous impact on the customs of our people here in Montgomery. It is not an easy thing to live under a law recognized as constitutional for these many years and then have it suddenly overturned on the basis of psychology. . . . The City Commission, and we know our people are with us in this determination, will not yield one inch, but will do all in its power to oppose the integration of the Negro race with the white race in Montgomery, and will forever stand like a rock against social equality, inter-marriage, and mixing of the races under God's creation and plan.

On December 20, the bus integration order finally reached Montgomery. A mass meeting was immediately scheduled for that evening, to give the people final instructions before returning to the buses the following day. I called Mr. Bagley, manager of the bus company, and asked him to be sure to have service restored on all of the major lines. With evident relief, he agreed.

To the overflow crowd at the St. John A.M.E. Church I read the following message that I had carefully prepared in the afternoon:

> For more than twelve months now, we, the Negro citizens of Montgomery, have been engaged in a nonviolent protest against injustices

and indignities experienced on city buses. We came to see that, in the long run, it is more honorable to walk in dignity than ride in humiliation. So in a quiet dignified manner, we decided to substitute tired feet for tired souls, and walk the streets of Montgomery until the sagging walls of injustice had been crushed. . . .

These twelve months have not been easy. Our feet have often been tired. We have struggled against tremendous odds to maintain alternative transportation. We can remember days when unfavorable court decisions came upon us like tidal waves, leaving us treading the waters of despair. But amid all of this we have kept going with the faith that as we struggle, God struggles with us, and that the arc of the moral universe, although long, is bending toward justice. We have lived under the agony and darkness of Good Friday with the conviction that one day the heightened glow of Easter would emerge on the horizon. We have seen truth crucified and goodness buried, but we have kept going with the conviction that truth crushed to earth will rise again.

Now our faith seems to be vindicated. This morning the long awaited mandate from the United States Supreme Court concerning bus segregation came to Montgomery. This mandate expresses in terms that are crystal clear that segregation in public transportation is both legally and sociologically invalid. In the light of this mandate and the unanimous vote rendered by the Montgomery Improvement Association about a month ago, the year-old protest against city buses is officially called off, and the Negro citizens of Montgomery are urged to return to the buses tomorrow morning on a nonsegregated basis.

I cannot close without giving just a word of caution. Our experience and growth during this past year of nonviolent protest has been such that we cannot be satisfied with a court "victory" over our white brothers. We must respond to the decision with an understanding of those who have oppressed us and with an appreciation of the new adjustments that the court order poses for them. We must be able to face up honestly to our own shortcomings. We must act in such a way as to make possible a coming together of white people and colored people on the basis of a real harmony of interests and understanding. We seek an integration based on mutual respect.

This is the time that we must evince calm dignity and wise restraint. Emotions must not run wild. Violence must not come from any of us, for if we become victimized with violent intents, we will have walked in vain, and our twelve months of glorious dignity will be transformed into an eve of gloomy catastrophe. As we go back to the buses let us be loving enough to turn an enemy into a friend. We must now move from protest to reconciliation. It is my firm conviction that God is working in Montgomery. Let all men of goodwill, both Negro and white, continue to work with Him. With this dedication we will be able to emerge from the bleak and desolate midnight of man's inhumanity to man to the bright and glittering daybreak of freedom and justice.

The audience stood and cheered loudly. This was the moment toward which they had pressed for more than a year. The return to the buses, on an integrated basis, was a new beginning. But it was a conclusion, too, the end of an effort that had drawn Montgomery's Negroes together as never before. To many of those present the joy was not unmixed. Some perhaps feared what might happen when they began to ride the buses again the next day. Others had found a spiritual strength in sacrifice to a cause; now the sacrifice was no longer necessary. Like many consummations, this one left a slight aftertaste of sadness.

At the close of the meeting I asked the ministers to stay over for a few minutes to urge them to ride the buses during the rush hours for the first few days. It was our feeling that their presence would give the Negro citizens courage and made them less likely to retaliate in case of insults. The ministers readily agreed. Accordingly, two were assigned to each bus line in the city, to ride mainly during the morning and afternoon rush. They were given suggestions as to how to handle situations of violence and urged to keep an accurate record of all incidents.

I had decided that after many months of struggling with my people for the goal of justice I should not sit back and watch, but should lead them back to the buses myself. I asked Ralph Abernathy, E. D. Nixon, and Glenn Smiley to join me in riding on the first integrated bus. They reached my house around 5:45 on Friday morning. Television cameras, photographers, and news reporters were hovering outside the door. At 5:55 we walked toward the bus stop, the cameras shooting, the reporters bombarding us with questions. Soon the bus appeared; the door opened, and I stepped on. The bus driver greeted me with a cordial smile. As I put my fare in the box he said:

"I believe you are Reverend King, aren't you?"

I answered: "Yes I am."

"We are glad to have you this morning," he said.

I thanked him and took my seat, smiling now too. Abernathy, Nixon, and Smiley followed, with several reporters and television men behind them. Glenn Smiley sat next to me. So I rode the first integrated bus in Montgomery with a white minister, and a native Southerner, as my seatmate.

Downtown we transferred to one of the buses that serviced the white residential section. As the white people boarded, many took seats as if nothing were going on. Others looked amazed to see Negroes sitting in front, and some appeared peeved to know that they either had to sit behind Negroes or stand. One elderly man stood up by the conductor, despite the fact that there were several vacant seats in the rear. When someone suggested to him that he sit in back, he responded: "I would rather die and go to hell than sit behind a nigger." A white woman unknowingly took a seat by a Negro. When she noticed her neighbor, she jumped up and said in a tone of obvious anger: "What are these niggers gonna do next?"

But despite such signs of hostility there were no major incidents on the first day. Many of the whites responded to the new system calmly. Several deliberately and with friendly smiles took seats beside Negroes. True, one Negro woman was slapped by a white man as she alighted, but she refused to retaliate. Later she said: "I could have broken that little fellow's neck all by myself, but I left the mass meeting last night determined to do what Reverend King asked." The *Montgomery Advertiser* reported at the end of the first day: "The calm but cautious acceptance of this significant change in Montgomery's way of life came without any major disturbance."

But the reactionaries were not in retreat. Many of them had predicted violence, and such predictions are always a conscious or unconscious invitation to action. When people, especially in public office, talk about bloodshed as a concomitant of integration, they stir and arouse the hoodlums to acts of destruction, and often work under cover to bring them about. In Montgomery several public officials had predicted violence, and violence there had to be if they were to save face.

By December 28 the first few days of peaceful compliance had given way to a reign of terror. City buses were fired on throughout the city, especially in poorly lighted sections. A teenage girl was beaten by four or five white men as she alighted from a bus. A pregnant Negro woman was shot in the leg. Fearfully, many Negroes and whites refused to ride the buses. The city commission responded by suspending the night runs on city lines. No bus could begin a run after five o'clock, which meant that once again returning workers were without transportation. This was exactly what the violent elements wanted.

During this period a new effort was made to divide the Negroes. Handbills were distributed urging Negroes to rebel against me in particular and their leaders in general. These leaflets purported to come from "fed-up" Negroes, but virtually everyone knew that they were the work of white extremists. Referring to me as Luther, one leaflet said: "We get shot at while he rides. He is getting us in more trouble every day. Wake up. Run him out of town." Another one stated: "We been doing OK in Montgomery before outside preachers were born! Ask Reverend King's papa & Mamma if they like his doings—ask him if they going to help in Atlanta. Better quit him before it is too late!"

The KKK was in its element. One day it descended upon Montgomery in full regalia. But it seemed to have lost its spell. A college student who saw the Klansmen swarming the streets in their white costumes with red insignia went cheerfully on about her business, thinking that they were collecting for the United Fund. And one cold night a small Negro boy was seen warming his hands at a burning cross.

On January 9, Ralph Abernathy and I went to Atlanta to prepare for a meeting of Negro leaders that I had called for the following day. In the middle of the night we were awakened by a telephone call from Ralph's wife, Juanita. I knew that only some new disaster would make her rouse us at two in the morning. When Ralph came back, his sober face told part of the story. "My home has been bombed," he said, "and three or four other explosions have been heard in the city, but Juanita doesn't know where yet." I asked about Juanita and their daughter. "Thank God, they are safe." Before we could talk any more, the telephone rang a second time. It was Juanita again, saying that the First Baptist Church had been hit. I looked at Ralph as he sat down beside me, stunned. Both his home and his church bombed in one night, and I knew no words to comfort him. There in the early morning hours we prayed to God together, asking for the power of endurance, the strength to carry on.

Between three and seven we received no less than fifteen calls. We finally learned that besides Ralph's home and church, Bob Graetz's home and three other Baptist churches—Bell Street,

Hutchinson Street, and Mt. Olive—had all been hit. Worrying that this time the people might be goaded into striking back, I called a few ministers in Montgomery and urged them to do what they could to keep control. In the meantime, Ralph and I arranged to fly back, leaving the meeting of Southern leaders to begin without us.

From the Montgomery airport we drove directly to Ralph's house. The street was roped off, and hundreds of people stood staring at the ruins. The front porch had been almost completely destroyed, and things inside the house were scattered from top to bottom. Juanita, though shocked and pale, was fairly composed.

The rest of the morning was spent in a grim tour of the other bombings. The Bell Street and Mt. Olive Baptist churches had been almost completely destroyed. The other two churches were less severely damaged, but nevertheless faced great losses. The total damage to the four churches was estimated at $70,000. Bob Graetz's home had been a bomb target the previous summer, but had escaped serious damage. This time he was not so fortunate. The front of his house lay in ruins, and shattered glass throughout the interior showed the violence of the explosion. Assembled at each of the bombed sites was a large group of angry people; but with a restraint that I never ceased to wonder at, they held themselves under control.

The next morning, three important white agencies issued statements condemning the bombings. Grover Hall, the editor of the *Montgomery Advertiser,* wrote a strong editorial entitled "Is it safe to live in Montgomery?" in which he insisted that the issue had gone beyond the question of segregation *versus* integration. As I read Hall's strong statement I could not help admiring this brilliant but complex man who claimed to be a supporter of segregation but could not stomach the excesses performed in its name. Several white ministers denounced the bombing as un-

christian and uncivilized, and all through the day their statement
was repeated over television by the distinguished minister of the
First Presbyterian Church, Rev. Merle Patterson. The Men of
Montgomery, too, made known their unalterable opposition to the
bombings. For the first time since the protest began, these influential whites were on public record on the side of law and order.
Their stands gave us new confidence in the basic decency of the
vast majority of whites in the community. Despite their commitment to segregation, it was clear that they were still law-
abiding, and would never sanction the use of violence to preserve
the system.

That afternoon, I returned to Atlanta to make at least an appearance at the meeting of Negro leaders. There I found an
enthusiastic group of almost a hundred men from all over the
South, committed to the idea of a Southern movement to implement the Supreme Court's decision against bus segregation
through nonviolent means. Before adjourning they voted to form
a permanent organization, the Southern Christian Leadership
Conference, and elected me president, a position I still hold.

When I returned to Montgomery over the weekend I found the
Negro community in low spirits. After the bombings the city
commission had ordered all buses off the streets; and it now appeared that the city fathers would use this reign of violence as an
excuse to cancel the bus company's franchise. As a result, many
were coming to feel that all our gains had been lost; and I myself
started to fear that we were in for another long struggle to get
bus service renewed. I was also beginning to wonder whether the
virulent leaflets that were bombarding the Negro community
might be having their effect. Discouraged, and still revolted by
the bombings, for some strange reason I began to feel a personal
sense of guilt for everything that was happening.

178 STRIDE TOWARD FREEDOM

In this mood I went to the mass meeting on Monday night. There for the first time, I broke down in public. I had invited the audience to join me in prayer, and had begun by asking God's guidance and direction in all our activities. Then, in the grip of an emotion I could not control, I said, "Lord, I hope no one will have to die as a result of our struggle for freedom in Montgomery. Certainly I don't want to die. But if anyone has to die, let it be me." The audience was in an uproar. Shouts and cries of "no, no" came from all sides. So intense was the reaction, that I could not go on with my prayer. Two of my fellow ministers came to the pulpit and suggested that I take a seat. For a few minutes I stood with their arms around me, unable to move. Finally, with the help of my friends, I sat down. It was this scene that caused the press to report mistakenly that I had collapsed.

Unexpectedly, this episode brought me great relief. Many people came up to me after the meeting and many called the following day to assure me that we were all together until the end. For the next few days, the city was fairly quiet. Bus service was soon resumed, though still on a daytime schedule only.

Then another wave of terror hit. Early in the morning of January 28, the People's Service Station and Cab Stand was bombed, and another bomb fell at the home of Allen Robertson, a sixty-year-old Negro hospital worker. It was never discovered why these two victims had been singled out for attack. The same morning an unexploded bomb, crudely assembled from twelve sticks of dynamite, was found still smoldering on my porch.

I was staying with friends on the other side of town, and Coretta and "Yoki" were in Atlanta. So once more I heard the news first on the telephone. On my way home, I visited the other scenes of disaster nearby, and found to my relief that no one had been hurt. I noticed a police car driving away from the area with two Negroes on the rear seat. These men, I learned, were under arrest because they had challenged the police to their faces with having done nothing to catch the bombers. Both were later convicted of trying to "incite to riot." But there was no riot that day, although the crowds that had gathered around the damaged buildings were once again ready for violence. They were just waiting for a signal. Fortunately, the signal never came.

At home I addressed the crowd from my porch, where the mark of the bomb was clear. "We must not return violence under any condition. I know this is difficult advice to follow, especially since we have been the victims of no less than ten bombings. But this is the way of Christ; it is the way of the cross. We must somehow believe that unearned suffering is redemptive." Then, since it was Sunday morning, I urged the people to go home and get ready for church. Gradually they dispersed.

With these bombings the community came to see that Montgomery was fast being plunged into anarchy. Finally, the city began to investigate in earnest. Rewards of $4000 were offered for information leading to the arrest and conviction of the bombers. On January 31, the Negro community was surprised to hear that seven white men had been arrested in connection with the bombings. Detective J. D. Shows was given credit for apprehending them.

All of the men were released on bonds ranging from $250 to $13,000, and the city court passed the charges to the Montgomery County Grand Jury without testimony. The Grand Jury indicted five of the men and dropped charges against the other two.

The trial of the first two defendants, Raymond D. York and Sonny Kyle Livingston, came up in the Montgomery County Court, the same court where I had been tried in the anti-boycott case a year before, and with the same solicitor, William F. Thetford, in charge of the prosecution. With the Emmet Till case in

Mississippi still fresh in our memories, the Negroes held little hope of conviction.

Several of us were subpoenaed as witnesses. On the opening day, we found the courtroom jammed with spectators, most of them white. In fact there was scarcely room for the Negroes. One could tell from the dress and manner of the whites that most of them were poor and uneducated, the kind that would find security in the Ku Klux Klan. As we entered they looked at us with undisguised hate.

The defense attorneys spent two days attempting to prove the innocence of their clients, arguing that the bombings had been carried out by the MIA in order to inspire new outside donations for their dwindling treasury. At the end of the second day I was called to the witness stand by the defense. For more than an hour I was questioned on things which had no relevance to the bombing case. The lawyers lifted statements of mine out of context to give the impression that I was a perpetrator of hate and violence. At many points they invented derogatory statements concerning white people, and attributed them to me.

On the other hand Mr. Thetford fought as diligently for a conviction as he had fought for mine a year earlier. He had an excellent case. The men had signed confessions. But in spite of all the evidence, the jury returned a verdict of not guilty. With their friends crowding around them, Raymond D. York and Sonny Kyle Livingston walked grinning out of the courtroom.

Justice had once more miscarried. But the diehards had made their last stand. The disturbances ceased abruptly. Desegregation on the buses proceeded smoothly. In a few weeks transportation was back to normal, and people of both races rode together wherever they pleased. The skies did not fall when integrated buses finally traveled the streets of Montgomery.

X

Montgomery Today

How are things in Montgomery today?" I am often asked. Everywhere I go people who have followed the reports of the bus protest in the newspapers or heard speakers tell about it wonder what the situation is now that bus desegregation has become a legal fact. They want to know whether the new pattern has been accepted by white as well as Negro residents of Montgomery, and whether there have been any other lasting effects of the great excitement that for over a year made the city front-page news throughout the nation and in many parts of the world.

At first, when this question was put to me, it was difficult to give a ready answer. Many things have to be considered in an appraisal of this sort, and not all of the effects are perceptible at once. But as the months passed after December 21, 1956, when bus segregation came to its official end, the answer became increasingly clear. "Better," I could say; "things are much better in Montgomery today."

On the buses Negroes, and white people too, now have the right to take any unoccupied seat anywhere. The younger Negroes —especially high school and college students—and the more educated and professional people exercise this new right freely.

NOTE: The author is grateful to Professor Lawrence Reddick of Alabama State College for his help in the preparation of this chapter.

On the other hand, many of the elderly Negroes and those who work in domestic service still tend to take a rear seat, partly from timidity, partly from habit born of custom. On the bus lines that serve predominantly white neighborhoods, Negroes generally retire to the rear. On lines that serve predominantly Negro neighborhoods, the whites seem to seat themselves close to the driver—or stand. Yet it is not unusual to see white people sitting behind Negro passengers. Seldom do Negro and white passengers share a double seat; there appears to be a mutual disinclination to do so. And yet a few such cases, too, have been noticed.

Considering the thousands who use the public transportation system daily, there have been surprisingly few conflicts on the buses. But there have been some. Harsh words have been exchanged between Negro and white passengers scrambling for seats. In one case a white man struck a Negro woman with a wrench. She and her two female companions, forgetting non-violence for the moment, overpowered him and struck him several sharp blows. The case went to court and the judge, fair-minded on this occasion, fined the man for disorderly conduct and did not even reprimand the women.

In another episode, a white woman claimed that a Negro man had attempted to take the seat beside her in order to get familiar with her. He was fined for disorderly conduct, although it appeared to be a case of her word against his. This was an isolated instance, however. More such situations had been expected, and some of us had feared that diehard opponents of desegregation might "plant" white women on buses so that they could make such complaints and stir up trouble. Happily, our fears were misplaced.

Long before the final court order came through, the Montgomery City Lines had given up their policy of racial segregation and had begun to school their employees in proper behavior with

all customers. The company removed from the buses all signs indi-
cating segregation. The drivers, who were perhaps the chief
irritants that "caused" the year-long protest, are no longer discour-
teous. Some of them are actively polite, saying "good morning"
to their regular riders. Although the bus company had indicated
at the end of the protest that they would be willing to accept
applications from Negro drivers, the agreement has not to this
day been put to the test.

We believe that our campaign of instruction and publicity
before the first day of our return to the buses was an important
factor in the comparative peace that followed. Our training sessions and mimeographed instructions had been successful in
driving home the slogan, "If pushed, don't push back; if cursed,
don't curse back." This time a soft answer did turn away wrath.
Moreover, our effort to convince white bus riders and the white
public in general that we did not intend to boast of our victory
or to take over the buses apparently got across. The white people,
knowing our attitude, had no reason to prepare for aggression or
to assume a stiff posture of defense.

Race relations are better too in the city at large. After the sharp
but brief flareup of bombings and shootings right after bus
desegregation, the violence of the extremists came to an abrupt
end. After the acquittal of the first two confessed bombers, the
remainder were set free in an amnesty that also canceled the cases
against the Negroes arrested under the anti-boycott law, with the
provision that I pay the $500 fine lodged against me in court.
I was reluctant to pay the fine, since such a step might appear to
imply acceptance for the unjust equation of our actions with the
brute violence of the bombers. Unfortunately, however, delay
in transcribing the testimony in my case had caused it to be
thrown out of court, which meant that any further legal action
would have to be based on technicalities rather than on the merits

of the issues. So I accepted the necessary compromise and paid.

Today the Negro citizen in Montgomery is respected in a way that he never was before. In the calm aftermath of the crisis many local white people are ready to say what they felt they could not afford to admit while the struggle was going on: "We've got to hand it to those Negroes. They had principles and they stuck to them and they stuck together. They organized and planned well." Others simply say, "We didn't think they had it in them." Again I believe that much of this residue of good will has come about because of our insistence on nonviolence. There are no white homes in Montgomery that have lost or injured ones as a result of racial clashes over the buses. Casualties of war keep alive postwar bitterness; fortunately Montgomery's whites have no such casualties.

In the downtown stores today the business of the Negro customer is appreciated and he is treated courteously in most places. It is no longer unusual to hear the Negro addressed as Mr. or Mrs. Even the Montgomery *Advertiser* now makes it a policy to use courtesy titles in references to Negroes in its pages.

The local labor movement has become somewhat more integrated than it was before the protest. Many union meetings are desegregated. And although there are also other factors at work, the improved general atmosphere may account in part for the election of eight Negroes to the joint AFL-CIO Executive Board for Southern Alabama.

Despite this picture of general improvement, it would be false to imply that the majority of white people in Montgomery have ceased to oppose integration. The opposite is closer to the truth. This city shares most of the fears of the state and the region, and there are still white citizens who react to the issue with all the raw emotions of patriots in a lost cause. Thus no move has yet been made to integrate the public schools in accordance with the now four-year-old directive of the United States Supreme Court. This is the big barrier currently erected. Here the segregationists seem determined to make an all-out stand. The rebels yell in Southern accents, "They shall not pass."

The two elements that are still most responsible for active segregationist sentiment are the newspapers and the politicians. Day in and day out the press is filled with stories of racial conflict, local and national. Any such disturbance in the North is played up here. Likewise the editorial pages constantly hammer at the Negro question. Readers are never permitted to forget that there is a war against "Yankees and race mixing."

The Alabama State Legislature, like most bodies of this sort in the Deep South, has passed many laws to delay or circumvent integration. Their effort to split up adjacent Macon County illustrates the extremes to which they are ready to go. In that county Negroes outnumber whites seven to one. If all eligibles were permitted to register and vote, the Negroes would inevitably share in some of the public offices. Moreover, Macon County contains the town where Booker T. Washington's famous Tuskegee Institute is located; there, thanks to Professor Charles Gomillion and the Tuskegee Civic Association, an energetic campaign for Negro registration and voting has been conducted. The State Legislature reacted first by redrawing the boundaries of Tuskegee so that almost all registered Negroes were outside the city limits; whereupon the Negroes instituted a boycott against the downtown stores that had supported or given tacit consent to the gerrymander. Next the governing body offered a referendum asking the voters of the state to authorize it, after due investigation, to split up Macon County itself, attaching slices to neighboring units, so that in every county of the area the white population would exceed the Negro. The voters assented, and the fate of Macon

County now hangs in the balance of the investigating committee. Such agitation right next door to Montgomery has had its effect here. In turn, the success of the Montgomery bus protest has helped inspire the disfranchised Negroes of Macon County to pursue their campaign vigorously but without violence.

The state struck another blow at the Negro cause when it succeeded in persuading the Circuit Court to issue a temporary injunction against the NAACP in Alabama. This injunction, which became effective in June 1956—at the same time that several NAACP lawyers were successfully fighting our case against bus segregation in federal court—is still in effect.

The city commissioners of Montgomery have also passed several anti-Negro measures. New city ordinances make it a crime for Negroes and whites to play together or participate jointly in any sport or game, even checkers, or to use the same parks or playgrounds. A few years ago Montgomery had one or two Negroes on the city's baseball team, the Montgomery Rebels; this would no longer be possible. In the meantime, however, the complaint at the box office of "poor local support" has caused the franchise of the Montgomery Rebels to be sold to Knoxville. Under the new ordinances, a Negro man was arrested recently for merely walking through a "white" park; and a Negro family on a visit to the city was arrested when the father stopped to let his children look at the caged animals in the "white" zoo.

But the local courts are no longer so certain of their role. They remember too well what happened to their rulings on bus segregation when the United States Supreme Court reviewed them. They fear that the high court could also knock out other forms of segregation in public facilities if such cases should make their way to Washington. Accordingly, the local court dismissed the case of the Negro who had walked through the park, when he apologized for his "error." Moreover, the charge entered against other violators of segregation law is now merely "disorderly conduct," thus avoiding the possibility of a test case for appeal to the highest court of the land.

Politicians still get their loudest cheers from white audiences when they pledge an all-out fight against integration, but the listeners seem to be less inclined to pay for these comforting words. The Ku Klux Klan is virtually impotent and openly denounced on all sides, although to some extent opposition to the Klan is simply a convenient screen, since the White Citizens Councils have taken over most of the KKK's major objectives. Yet even the Councils appear to be slipping in Montgomery. Contributions have steadily declined since bus integration became a reality. That such organizations could not prevent this from happening was evidence to many of the dues-paying members that they could best use their own dollars otherwise.

Meanwhile, what of Montgomery's Negro community? Here too the experience of the protest has had its lasting and beneficial effects. Although the intense solidarity of the protest year has inevitably attenuated, there is still a feeling of closeness among the various classes and ages and religious denominations that was never present before. The increased self-respect of even the least sophisticated Negroes in Montgomery is evident in the way they dress and walk, in new standards of cleanliness and of general deportment. As one Negro janitor told a reporter from the North: "We got our heads up now, and we won't ever bow down again —no, sir—except before God!"

There has been a decline in heavy drinking. Statistics on crime and divorce indicate that both are on the wane. A nurse who owns a Negro hospital in Montgomery says that since the protest she has been able to go to church on Sunday mornings, something she had not been able to do for years. This means that

Saturday nights are less belligerent than they used to be. There is a contagious spirit of friendliness and warmth; even the children seem to display a new sense of belonging.

The MIA has reduced its budget and staff, but it has broadened its focus and begun to address itself to other large areas of civic improvement. It has retained Fred Gray as full-time legal counsel to handle civil rights cases. It continues to conduct the once-a-week mass meetings, where, besides the religious program, voting clinics are held, and the speaker of the evening discusses the news and current issues of interest. Preceding the meetings a well-attended program of adult education demonstrates the Negroes' new concern with self-improvement.

The MIA has set forth a ten-point program entitled "Looking Forward," which envisions efforts in the fields of civic and political education, community relations, education for individual competence, improvement of economic status, health, recreation, law enforcement, public relations, cultural advancement, and spiritual enrichment. Parts of this long-range program are still on the drawing board; others are already in operation. Of most immediate importance, perhaps, is the continuing effort to promote registration and voting among all Negroes of voting age. This is still an arduous task; thanks chiefly to the persistent opposition of the white registrars, of the nearly 2000 Negroes sent to register locally in the last two years, barely 10 per cent have succeeded in getting their names on the books of eligible voters.

Thus Montgomery's racial problems are still far from solved. Yet it is clear that things are much better than they were before December 5, 1955. Citizens have more mutual respect and more respect for themselves. Above all, our experience has shown that social change can take place without violence.

XI

Where Do We Go From Here?

T HE bus struggle in Montgomery, Alabama, is now history. As the integrated buses roll daily through the city they carry, along with their passengers, a meaning-crowded symbolism. Accord among the great majority of passengers is evidence of the basic good will of man for man and a portent of peace in the desegregated society to come. Occasional instances of discord among passengers are a reminder that in other areas of Montgomery life segregation yet obtains with all of its potential for group strife and personal conflict. Indeed, segregation is still a reality throughout the South.

Where do we go from here? Since the problem in Montgomery is merely symptomatic of the larger national problem, where do we go not only in Montgomery but all over the South and the nation? Forces maturing for years have given rise to the present crisis in race relations. What are these forces that have brought the crisis about? What will be the conclusion? Are we caught in a social and political impasse, or do we have at our disposal the creative resources to achieve the ideals of brotherhood and harmonious living?

The last half century has seen crucial changes in the life of the American Negro. The social upheavals of the two world wars, the great depression, and the spread of the automobile have made it both possible and necessary for the Negro to move away from his former isolation on the rural plantation. The decline of agriculture and the parallel growth of industry have drawn large numbers of Negroes to urban centers and brought about a gradual improvement in their economic status. New contacts have led to a broadened outlook and new possibilities for educational advance. All of these factors have conjoined to cause the Negro to take a fresh look at himself. His expanding life experiences have created within him a consciousness that he is an equal element in a larger social compound and accordingly should be given rights and privileges commensurate with his new responsibilities. Once plagued with a tragic sense of inferiority resulting from the crippling effects of slavery and segregation, the Negro has now been driven to reëvaluate himself. He has come to feel that he is somebody. His religion reveals to him that God loves all His children and that the important thing about a man is not "his specificity but his fundamentum"—not the texture of his hair or the color of his skin but his eternal worth to God.

This growing self-respect has inspired the Negro with a new determination to struggle and sacrifice until first-class citizenship becomes a reality. This is the true meaning of the Montgomery Story. One can never understand the bus protest in Montgomery without understanding that there is a new Negro in the South, with a new sense of dignity and destiny.

Along with the Negro's changing image of himself has come an awakening moral consciousness on the part of millions of white Americans concerning segregation. Ever since the signing of the Declaration of Independence, America has manifested a schizophrenic personality on the question of race. She has been torn between selves—a self in which she has proudly professed democracy and a self in which she has sadly practiced the antithesis of democracy. The reality of segregation, like slavery, has always had to confront the ideals of democracy and Christianity. Indeed, segregation and discrimination are strange paradoxes in a nation founded on the principle that all men are created equal. This contradiction has disturbed the consciences of whites both North and South, and has caused many of them to see that segregation is basically evil.

Climaxing this process was the Supreme Court's decision outlawing segregation in the public schools. For all men of good will May 17, 1954, marked a joyous end to the long night of enforced segregation. In unequivocal language the Court affirmed that "separate but equal" facilities are inherently unequal, and that to segregate a child on the basis of his race is to deny that child equal protection of the law. This decision brought hope to millions of disinherited Negroes who had formerly dared only to dream of freedom. It further enhanced the Negro's sense of dignity and gave him even greater determination to achieve justice.

This determination of Negro Americans to win freedom from all forms of oppression springs from the same deep longing that motivates oppressed peoples all over the world. The rumblings of discontent in Asia and Africa are expressions of a quest for freedom and human dignity by people who have long been the victims of colonialism and imperialism. So in a real sense the racial crisis in America is a part of the larger world crisis.

But the numerous changes which have culminated in a new sense of dignity on the part of the Negro are not of themselves responsible for the present crisis. If all men accepted these historical changes in good faith there would be no crisis. The crisis developed when the collective pressures to achieve fair goals for the Negro met with tenacious and determined resistance. Then the emerging new order, based on the principle of democratic equalitarianism, came face to face with the older order, based on the principles of paternalism and subordination. The crisis was not produced by outside agitators, NAACP'ers, Montgomery Protesters, or even the Supreme Court. The crisis developed, paradoxically, when the most sublime principles of American democracy—imperfectly realized for almost two centuries—began fulfilling themselves and met with the brutal resistance of forces seeking to contract and repress freedom's growth.

The resistance has risen at times to ominous proportions. Many states have reacted in open defiance. The legislative halls of the South still ring loud with such words as "interposition" and "nullification." Many public officials are using the power of their offices to defy the law of the land. Through their irresponsible actions, their inflammatory statements, and their dissemination of distortions and half-truths, they have succeeded in arousing abnormal fears and morbid antipathies within the minds of under-privileged and uneducated whites, leaving them in such a state of excitement and confusion that they are led to acts of meanness and violence that no normal person would commit.

This resistance to the emergence of the new order expresses itself in the resurgence of the Ku Klux Klan. Determined to pre-serve segregation at any cost, this organization employs methods that are crude and primitive. It draws its members from under-privileged groups who see in the Negro's rising status a political and economic threat. Although the Klan is impotent politically and openly denounced from all sides, it remains a dangerous force which thrives on racial and religious bigotry. Because of its past history, whenever the Klan moves there is fear of violence.

Then there are the White Citizens Councils. Since they occa-sionally recruit members from a higher social and economic level than the Klan, a halo of partial respectability hovers over them. But like the Klan they are determined to preserve segregation despite the law. Their weapons of threat, intimidation, and boy-cott are directed both against Negroes and against any whites who stand for justice. They demand absolute conformity from white and abject submission from Negroes. The Citizens Councils often argue piously that they abhor violence, but their defiance of the law, their unethical methods, and their vitriolic public pronouncements inevitably create the atmosphere in which violence thrives.

As a result of the Councils' activities most white moderates in the South no longer feel free to discuss in public the issues involved in desegregation for fear of social ostracism and economic reprisals. What channels of communication had once existed between whites and Negroes have thus now been largely closed.

The present crisis in race relations has characteristics that come to the forefront in any period of social transition. The guardians of the status quo lash out with denunciation against the person or organization that they consider most responsible for the emergence of the new order. Often this denunciation rises to major proportions. In the transition from slavery to restricted emancipation Abraham Lincoln was assassinated. In the present transition from segregation to desegregation the Supreme Court is castigated and the NAACP is maligned and subjected to extralegal reprisals.

As in other social crises the defenders of the status quo in the South argue that they were gradually solving their own problems until external pressure was brought to bear upon them. The familiar complaint in the South today is that the Supreme Court's decision on education has set us back a generation in race relations, that people of different races who had long lived at peace have now been turned against one another. But this is a misinterpretation of what is taking place. When a subject people moves toward freedom, they are not creating a cleavage, but are revealing the cleavage which apologists of the old order have sought to conceal. It is not the movement for integration which is creating a cleavage in the United States today. The depth of the cleavage that existed, the true nature of which the moderates failed to see and make clear, is being revealed by the resistance to integration.

During a crisis period, a desperate attempt is made by the extremists to influence the minds of the liberal forces in the ruling majority. So, for example, in the present transition white Southerners attempt to convince Northern whites that the Negroes are inherently criminal. They seek instances of Negro crime and juvenile delinquency in Northern communities and then say: "You see, the Negroes are problems to you. They create problems wherever they go." The accusation is made without reference to the true nature of the situation. Environmental problems of delinquency are interpreted as evidence of racial criminality. Crises arising in Northern schools are interpreted as proofs that Negroes are inherently delinquent. The extremists do not recognize that these school problems are symptoms of urban dislocation, rather than expressions of racial deficiency. Criminality and delinquency are not racial; poverty and ignorance breed crime whatever the racial group may be.

In the attempt to influence the minds of Northern and Southern liberals, the segregationists are often subtle and skillful. Those who are too smart to argue for the validity of segregation and racial inferiority on the basis of the Bible set forth their arguments on cultural and sociological grounds. The Negro is not ready for integration, they say; because of academic and cultural lags on the part of the Negro, the integration of schools will pull the white race down. They are never honest enough to admit that the academic and cultural lags in the Negro community are themselves the result of segregation and discrimination. The best way to solve any problem is to remove its cause. It is both rationally unsound and sociologically untenable to use the tragic effects of segregation as an argument for its continuation.

All of these calculated patterns—the defiance of Southern legislative bodies, the activities of White Supremacy organizations, and the distortions and rationalizations of the segregationists—have mounted up to massive resistance. This resistance grows out of the desperate attempt of the white South to perpetuate a system of human values that came into being under a feudalistic plantation system and which cannot survive in a day of growing urbanization and industrial expansion. These are the rock-bottom elements of the present crisis.

The schools of the South are the present storm center. Here the forces that stand for the best in our national life have been tragically ineffectual. A year after the Supreme Court had declared school segregation unconstitutional, it handed down a decree outlining the details by which integration should proceed "with all deliberate speed." While the Court did not set a definite deadline for the termination of this process, it did set a time for the beginning. It was clear that the Court had chosen this reasonable approach with the expectation that the forces of good will would immediately get to work and prepare the communities for a smooth and peaceful transition.

But the forces of good will failed to come through. The Office of the President was appallingly silent, though just an occasional word from this powerful source, counseling the nation on the moral aspects of integration and the need for complying with the law, might have saved the South from much of its present confusion and terror. Other forces of justice also failed to act. It is true that immediately after the first decision was rendered, leading church, labor, and social welfare leaders issued statements upholding the decision, and many supporting resolutions were adopted by their organizations. But hardly a single group set forth an action program wherein their members could actively work to bring about a peaceable transition. Neither did they develop a plan whereby individuals in Southern communities who were willing to work for desegregation could receive organization support in the face of economic reprisals and physical violence.

As a result of the failure of the moral forces of the nation to mobilize behind school integration, the forces of defeat were given the chance to organize and crystallize their opposition. While the good people stood silently and complacently by, the misguided people acted. If every church and synagogue had developed an action program; if every civic and social welfare organization, every labor union and educational institution, had worked out concrete plans for implementing their righteous resolutions; if the press, radio, and television had turned their powerful instruments in the direction of educating and elevating the people on this issue; if the President and the Congress had taken a forthright stand; if these things had happened, federal troops might not have been forced to walk the corridors of Central High School.

But it is still not too late to act. Every crisis has both its dangers and opportunities. It can spell either salvation or doom. In the present crisis America can achieve either racial justice or the ultimate social psychosis that can only lead to domestic suicide. The democratic ideal of freedom and equality will be fulfilled for all—or all human beings will share in the resulting social and spiritual doom. In short, this crisis has the potential for democracy's fulfillment or fascism's triumph; for social progress or retrogression. We can choose either to walk the high road of human brotherhood or to tread the low road of man's inhumanity to man.

History has thrust upon our generation an indescribably important destiny—to complete a process of democratization which our nation has too long developed too slowly, but which is our most powerful weapon for world respect and emulation. How we deal with this crucial situation will determine our moral health as individuals, our cultural health as a region, our political health as a nation, and our prestige as a leader of the free world. The future of America is bound up with the solution of the present crisis. The shape of the world today does not permit us the luxury of a faltering democracy. The United States cannot hope to attain the respect of the vital and growing colored nations of the world unless it remedies its racial problems at home. If America is to remain a first-class nation, it cannot have a second-class citizenship.

A solution of the present crisis will not take place unless men and women work for it. Human progress is neither automatic nor inevitable. Even a superficial look at history reveals that no social advance rolls in on the wheels of inevitability. Every step toward the goal of justice requires sacrifice, suffering, and struggle; the tireless exertions and passionate concern of dedicated individuals. Without persistent effort, time itself becomes an ally of the insurgent and primitive forces of irrational emotionalism and social destruction. This is no time for apathy or complacency. This is a time for vigorous and positive action.

It is the shame of the sunshine patriots if the foregoing paragraphs have a hollow sound, like an echo of countless political speeches. These things must be repeated time and again, for men forget quickly; but once said, they must be followed with a dynamic program, or else they become a refuge for those who shy from any action. If America is to respond creatively to the present crisis, many groups and agencies must rise above the reiteration of generalities and begin to take an active part in changing the face of their nation.

First, there is need for strong and aggressive leadership from the federal government. If the executive and legislative branches were as concerned about the protection of the citizenship rights of all people as the federal courts have been, the transition from a segregated to an integrated society would be much further along than it is today. The dearth of positive leadership from Washington is not confined to one political party. Both major parties have lagged in the service of justice. Many Democrats have betrayed it by capitulating to the undemocratic practices of the Southern Dixiecrats. Many Republicans have betrayed it by capitulating to the hypocrisy of right-wing Northerners.

In spite of the crucial role of the federal judiciary in this tense period of transition, the courts cannot do the job alone. The courts can clarify constitutional principles and remove the legal basis for segregation, but they cannot write laws, appoint administrators, or enforce justice on the local level.

The states and localities have the powers if they choose to exercise them. But the Southern states have made their policy clear. States' rights, they say in effect, include the right to abrogate power when it involves distasteful responsibilities, even to the Constitution of the United States, its amendments, and its judicial interpretation. So the power and the responsibility return by default to the federal government. It is up to all branches of the central government to accept the challenge.

Government action is not the whole answer to the present crisis, but it is an important partial answer. Morals cannot be legislated, but behavior can be regulated. The law cannot make an employer love me, but it can keep him from refusing to hire me because of the color of my skin. We must depend on religion and education to alter the errors of the heart and mind; but meanwhile it is an immoral act to compel a man to accept injustice until another man's heart is set straight. As the experience of several Northern states has shown, anti-discrimination laws can provide powerful sanctions against this kind of immorality.

Moreover, the law itself is a form of education. The words of the Supreme Court, of Congress, and of the Constitution are eloquent instructors. In fact, it would be a mistake to minimize the impact upon the South of the federal court orders and legislative and executive acts already in effect. Desegregation of the armed services, for instance, has already had an immense, incalculable impact. Federal court decrees have altered transportation patterns, teachers' salaries, the use of recreational facilities, and myriad other matters. The habits if not the hearts of people have been and are being altered every day by federal action.

Another group with a vital role to play in the present crisis is the white Northern liberals. The racial issue that we confront in America is not a sectional but a national problem. The citizenship rights of Negroes cannot be flouted anywhere without impairing the rights of every other American. Injustice anywhere is a threat to justice everywhere. A breakdown of law in Alabama weakens the very foundations of lawful government in the other forty-seven states. The mere fact that we live in the United States means that we are caught in a network of inescapable mutuality. Therefore, no American can afford to be apathetic about the problem of racial justice. It is a problem that meets every man at his front door. The racial problem will be solved in America to the degree that every American considers himself personally confronted with it. Whether one lives in the heart of the Deep South or on the periphery of the North, the problem of injustice is his problem; it is his problem because it is America's problem.

There is a pressing need for a liberalism in the North which is truly liberal, a liberalism that firmly believes in integration in its own community as well as in the Deep South. It is one thing to agree that the goal of integration is morally and legally right; it is another thing to commit oneself positively and actively to the ideal of integration—the former is intellectual assent, the latter is actual belief. These are days that demand practices to match professions. This is no day to pay lip service to integration, we must pay *life* service to it.

Today in all too many Northern communities a sort of quasi-liberalism prevails, so bent on seeing all sides that it fails to become dedicated to any side. It is so objectively analytical that it is not subjectively committed. A true liberal will not be deterred by the propaganda and subtle words of those who say, "Slow up for a while; you are pushing things too fast." I am not calling for an end to sympathetic understanding and abiding patience; but neither sympathy nor patience should be used as excuses for indecisiveness. They must be guiding principles for all of our actions, rather than substitutes for action itself.

A significant role, in this tense period of transition, is assigned to the moderates of the white South. Unfortunately today, the leadership of the white South is by and large in the hands of close-minded extremists. These persons gain prominence and power by the dissemination of false ideas, and by appealing to the deepest fears and hates within the human mind. But they do not speak for the South; of that I am convinced. They speak only for a willful and vocal minority.

Even the most casual observer can see that the South has marvelous possibilities. It is rich in natural resources, blessed with the beauties of nature, and endowed with a native warmth of spirit. Yet in spite of these assets, it is retarded by a blight that debilitates not only the Negro but also the white man. Poor white men, women, and children, bearing the scars of ignorance, deprivation, and poverty, are evidence of the fact that harm to one is injury to all. Segregation has placed the whole South socially, educationally, and economically behind the rest of the nation.

Yet actually, there is no single "solid" South; there are at least three, geographically speaking. There is the South of compliance —Oklahoma, Kentucky, Kansas, Missouri, West Virginia, Delaware, and the District of Columbia. There is the wait-and-see South—Tennessee, Texas, North Carolina, Arkansas, and Florida. And there is the South of resistance—Georgia, Alabama, Mississippi, Louisiana, South Carolina, and Virginia.

Just as there are three Souths geographically, there are several Souths in terms of attitudes. A minority in each of these states would use almost any means, including physical violence, to preserve segregation. A majority, through tradition and custom, sincerely believe in segregation, but at the same time stand on the side of law and order. Hence, they are willing to comply with the law not because they feel it is sound but because it is the law. A third group, a growing minority, is working courageously and conscientiously to implement the law of the land. These people believe in the morality as well as the constitutionality of integration. Their still small voices often go unheard among the louder shouts of defiance, but they are actively in the field.

Furthermore there are in the white South millions of people of good will whose voices are yet unheard, whose course is yet unclear, and whose courageous acts are yet unseen. These persons are often silent today because of fear—fear of social, political, and economic reprisals. In the name of God, in the interest of human dignity, and for the cause of democracy these millions are called upon to gird their courage, to speak out, to offer the leadership that is needed. Still another South calls upon them: The colored South, the South of millions of Negroes whose sweat and blood has also built Dixie, who yearn for brotherhood and respect, who want to join hands with their white fellow Southerners to build a freer, happier land for all. If the moderates of the white South fail to act now, history will have to record that the greatest tragedy of this period of social transition was not the strident clamor of the bad people, but the appalling silence of the good people. Our generation will have to repent not only for the acts and words of the children of darkness but also for the fears and apathy of the children of light.

Who can best lead the South out of the social and economic quagmire? Her native sons. Those who were born and bred on her rich and fertile soil; those who love her because they were nurtured by her. Through love, patience, and understanding good will they can call their brothers to a way of noble living. This hour represents a great opportunity for the white moderates, if they will only speak the truth, obey the law, and suffer if necessary for what they know is right.

Still another agency of effective change today is the labor movement. Across the years the Negro has been a perpetual victim of economic exploitation. Prior to the Civil War the slaves worked under a system which offered neither compensation nor civil rights. Since emancipation the Negro American has continued to suffer under an essentially unreconstructed economy. He was freed without land or legal protection, and was made an outcast entitled only to the most menial jobs. Even the federal government that set him free failed to work out any long-range policy that would guarantee economic resources to a previously enslaved people—as much entitled to the land they had worked as were their former owners. The exploitation of the Negro population persisted through the Reconstruction period and continues down to the present day.

Labor unions can play a tremendous role in making economic justice a reality for the Negro. Trade unions are engaged in a struggle to advance the economic welfare of those American citizens whose wages are their livelihood. Since the American Negro is virtually nonexistent as the owner and manager of mass production industry, he must depend on the payment of wages for his economic survival.

There are in the United States 16.5 million members of approximately 150 bona fide trade unions. Of this number 142 are national and international affiliated organizations of the AFL-CIO. The unions forming the AFL-CIO include 1.3 million Negroes among their 13.5 million members. Only the combined religious institutions serving the Negro community can claim a greater membership of Negroes. The Negro then has the right to expect the resources of the American trade union movement to be used in assuring him—like all the rest of its members—of a proper place in American society. He has gained this right along with all the other workers whose mutual efforts have built this country's free and democratic trade unions.

Economic insecurity strangles the physical and cultural growth of its victims. Not only are millions deprived of formal education and proper health facilities but our most fundamental social unit —the family—is tortured, corrupted, and weakened by economic insufficiency. When a Negro man is inadequately paid, his wife must work to provide the simple necessities for the children. When a mother has to work she does violence to motherhood by depriving her children of her loving guidance and protection; often they are poorly cared for by others or by none—left to roam the streets unsupervised. It is not the Negro alone who is wronged by a disrupted society; many white families are in similar straits. The Negro mother leaves home to care for—and be a substitute mother for—white children, while the white mother works. In this strange irony lies the promise of future correction.

Both Negro and white workers are equally oppressed. For

both, the living standards need to be raised to levels consistent with our national resources. Not logic but a hollow social distinction has separated the races. The economically depressed white accepts his poverty by telling himself that, if in no other respect, at least socially he is above the Negro. For this empty pride in a racial myth he has paid the crushing price of insecurity, hunger, ignorance, and hopelessness for himself and his children.

Strong ties must be made between those whites and Negroes who have problems in common. White and Negro workers have mutual aspirations for a fairer share of the products of industries and farms. Both seek job security, old-age security, health and welfare protection. The organized labor movement, which has contributed so much to the economic security and well-being of millions, must concentrate its powerful forces on bringing economic emancipation to white and Negro by organizing them together in social equality.

Certainly the labor movement has already made significant moves in this direction. Virtually every national or international union has clear policies of nondiscrimination, and the national leaders of AFL-CIO have proclaimed sincerely the ultimate objective of eliminating racial bias not only from the American labor movement but also from American society as a whole. But in spite of this stand, some unions, governed by the racist ethos, have contributed to the degraded economic status of the Negroes. Negroes have been barred from membership in certain unions, and denied apprenticeship training and vocational education. In every section of the country one can find local unions existing as a serious and vicious obstacle when the Negro seeks jobs or upgrading in employment. The AFL-CIO drive to organize the South has been virtually abandoned because of the massive resistance of a significant portion of the organized labor oligarchy, many of whom have been active in White Citizens Councils.

The existence of these conditions within the ranks of labor reveals that the job is a continuing one. The AFL-CIO must use all of the powerful forces at its command to enforce the principles it has professed. Labor leaders must continue to recognize that labor has a great stake in the struggle for civil rights, if only because the forces that are anti-Negro are usually anti-labor too. The current attacks on organized labor because of the misdeeds of a few malefactors should not blind us to labor's essential role in the present crisis.

The church too must face its historic obligation in this crisis. In the final analysis the problem of race is not a political but a moral issue. Indeed, as the Swedish economist Gunnar Myrdal has pointed out, the problem of race is America's greatest moral dilemma. This tragic dilemma presents the church with a great challenge. The broad universalism standing at the center of the gospel makes segregation morally unjustifiable. Racial segregation is a blatant denial of the unity which we have in Christ; for in Christ there is neither Jew nor Gentile, bond nor free, Negro nor white. Segregation scars the soul of both the segregator and the segregated. The segregator looks upon the segregated as a thing to be used, not a person to be respected. Segregation substitutes an "I-it" relationship for the "I-thou" relationship. Thus it is utterly opposed to the noble teachings of our Judeo-Christian tradition.

It has always been the responsibility of the church to broaden horizons, challenge the status quo, and break the mores when necessary. The task of conquering segregation is an inescapable *must* confronting the church today.

There are several specific things that the church can do. First, it should try to get to the ideational roots of race hate, something that the law cannot accomplish. All race prejudice is based upon fears, suspicions, and misunderstandings, usually groundless. The church can be of immeasurable help in giving the popular mind direction here. Through its channels of religious education, the church can point out the irrationality of these beliefs. It can show that the idea of a superior or inferior race is a myth that has been completely refuted by anthropological evidence. It can show that Negroes are not innately inferior in academic, health, and moral standards. It can show that, when given equal opportunities, Negroes can demonstrate equal achievement.

The church can also do a great deal to reveal the true intentions of the Negro—that he is not seeking to dominate the nation, but simply wants the right to live as a first-class citizen, with all the responsibilities that good citizenship entails. The church can also help by mitigating the prevailing and irrational fears concerning intermarriage. It can say to men that marriage is an individual matter that must be decided on the merits of individual cases. Properly speaking, races do not marry; individuals marry. Marriage is a condition which requires the voluntary consent of two contracting parties, and either side can always say no. The church can reveal that the continual outcry concerning intermarriage is a distortion of the real issue. It can point out that the Negro's primary aim is to be the white man's brother, not his brother-in-law.

Another thing that the church can do to make the principle of brotherhood a reality is to keep men's minds and visions centered on God. Many of the problems America now confronts can be explained in terms of fear. There is not only the job of freeing the Negro from the bondage of segregation but also the responsibility of freeing his white brothers from the bondage of fears concerning integration. One of the best ways to rid oneself of fear is to center one's life in the will and purpose of God. "Perfect love casteth out fear."

When people think about race problems they are too often more concerned with men than with God. The question usually asked is: "What will my friends think if I am too friendly to Negroes or too liberal on the race question?" Men forget to ask: "What will God think?" And so they live in fear because they tend to seek social approval on the horizontal plane rather than spiritual devotion on the vertical plane.

The church must remind its worshipers that man finds greater security in devoting his life to the eternal demands of the Almighty God than in giving his ultimate allegiance to the transitory demands of man. The church must continually say to Christians, "Ye are a colony of heaven." True, man has a dual citizenry. He lives both in time and in eternity; both in heaven and on earth. But he owes his ultimate allegiance to God. It is this love for God and devotion to His will that casteth out fear.

A further effort that the church can make in attempting to solve the race problem is to take the lead in social reform. It is not enough for the church to be active in the realm of ideas; it must move out into the arena of social action. First, the church must remove the yoke of segregation from its own body. Only by doing this can it be effective in its attack on outside evils. Unfortunately, most of the major denominations still practice segregation in local churches, hospitals, schools, and other church institutions. It is appalling that the most segregated hour of Christian America is eleven o'clock on Sunday morning, the same hour when many are standing to sing, "In Christ there is no East nor West." Equally appalling is the fact that the most segregated school of the week is the Sunday School. How often the church has had a high blood count of creeds and an anemia of deeds! Dean Liston Pope of the Yale Divinity School rightly says in *The Kingdom beyond Caste:* "The church is the most segregated major institution in American society. It has lagged behind

the Supreme Court as the conscience of the nation on questions
of race, and it has fallen far behind trade unions, factories,
schools, department stores, athletic gatherings and most other
major areas of human association as far as the achievement of
integration in its own life is concerned."

There has been some progress. Here and there churches are
courageously making attacks on segregation, and actually integrating their congregations. The National Council of Churches
has repeatedly condemned segregation and has requested its
constituent denominations to do likewise. Most of the major
denominations have endorsed that action. The Roman Catholic
Church has declared, "Segregation is morally wrong and sinful."
All this is admirable. But these stands are still far too few, and
they move all too slowly down to the local churches in actual
practice. The church has a schism in its own soul that it must
close. It will be one of the tragedies of Christian history if a
future Gibbon is able to say that at the height of the twentieth
century the church proved to be one of the greatest bulwarks of
segregated power.

The church must also become increasingly active in social
action outside its doors. It must seek to keep channels of communication open between the Negro and white community. It
must take an active stand against the injustice that Negroes confront in housing, education, police protection, and in city and state
courts. It must exert its influence in the area of economic justice.
As guardian of the moral and spiritual life of the community the
church cannot look with indifference upon these glaring evils.

It is impossible to speak of the role of the church without referring to the ministers. Every minister of the gospel has a mandate to stand up courageously for righteousness, to proclaim the
eternal verities of the gospel, and to lead men from the darkness
of falsehood and fear to the light of truth and love.

In the South this mandate presents white ministers with a difficult choice. Many who believe segregation to be directly opposed to the will of God and the spirit of Christ are faced with the painful alternative of taking a vocal stand and being fired or staying quiet in order to remain in the situation and do some good. Pastors who have adopted the latter course feel that if they were forced out of their churches their successors would in all probability be segregationist, thus setting the Christian cause back. Many ministers have kept their peace not merely to save a job but because they feel that restraint is the best way to serve the cause of Christ in the South. In quiet unpublicized ways many of these ministers are making for a better day and helpfully molding the minds of young people. These men should not be criticized.

In the final analysis every white minister in the South must decide for himself which course he will follow. There is no single right strategy. The important thing is for every minister to dedicate himself to the Christian ideal of brotherhood, and be sure that he is doing something positive to implement it. He must never allow the theory that it is better to remain quiet and help the cause to become a rationalization for doing nothing. Many ministers can do much more than they are doing and still hold their congregations. There is a great deal that ministers can achieve collectively. In every Southern city there should be interracial ministerial associations in which Negro and white ministers can come together in Christian fellowship and discuss common community problems. One of the most disappointing experiences of the Montgomery struggle was the fact that we could not get the white ministerial association to sit down with us and discuss our problem. With individual exceptions the white ministers, from whom I had naïvely expected so much, gave little.

Ministers can also collectively call for compliance with the law and a cessation of violence. This has been done by white ministers of Atlanta, Richmond, Dallas, and other cities, and not a single one has, to my knowledge, lost his job. It is difficult for a denomination to fire all of its ministers in a city. If ever the white ministers of the South decide to declare in a united voice the truth of the gospel on the question of race, the transition from a segregated to an integrated society will be infinitely smoother.

Any discussion of the role of the Christian minister today must ultimately emphasize the need for prophecy. Not every minister can be a prophet, but some must be prepared for the ordeals of this high calling and be willing to suffer courageously for righteousness. May the problem of race in America soon make hearts burn so that prophets will rise up, saying, "Thus saith the Lord," and cry out as Amos did, ". . . let justice roll down like waters, and righteousness like an ever-flowing stream."

Fortunately, a few in the South have already been willing to follow this prophetic way. I have nothing but praise for these ministers of the gospel of Jesus Christ and rabbis of the Jewish faith who have stood unflinchingly before threats and intimidations, inconvenience and unpopularity, even at times in physical danger, to declare the doctrine of the Fatherhood of God and the brotherhood of man. For such noble servants of God there is the consolation of the words of Jesus: "Blessed are ye, when men shall revile you, and persecute you, and shall say all manner of evil against you falsely, for my sake. Rejoice, and be exceeding glad: for great is your reward in heaven: for so persecuted they the prophets which were before you."

Here, then, is the hard challenge and the sublime opportunity: to let the spirit of Christ work toward fashioning a truly great

Christian nation. If the church accepts the challenge with devotion and valor, the day will be speeded when men everywhere will recognize that they "are all one in Christ Jesus."

Finally, the Negro himself has a decisive role to play if integration is to become a reality. Indeed, if first-class citizenship is to become a reality for the Negro he must assume the primary responsibility for making it so. Integration is not some lavish dish that the federal government or the white liberal will pass out on a silver platter while the Negro merely furnishes the appetite. One of the most damaging effects of past segregation on the personality of the Negro may well be that he has been victimized with the delusion that others should be more concerned than himself about his citizenship rights.

In this period of social change, the Negro must come to see that there is much he himself can do about his plight. He may be uneducated or poverty-stricken, but these handicaps must not prevent him from seeing that he has within his being the power to alter his fate. The Negro can take direct action against injustice without waiting for the government to act or a majority to agree with him or a court to rule in his favor.

Oppressed people deal with their oppression in three characteristic ways. One way is acquiescence: the oppressed resign themselves to their doom. They tacitly adjust themselves to oppression, and thereby become conditioned to it. In every movement toward freedom some of the oppressed prefer to remain oppressed. Almost 2800 years ago Moses set out to lead the children of Israel from the slavery of Egypt to the freedom of the promised land. He soon discovered that slaves do not always welcome their deliverers. They become accustomed to being slaves. They would rather bear those ills they have, as Shake-

speare pointed out, than flee to others that they know not of.
They prefer the "fleshpots of Egypt" to the ordeals of emancipation.

There is such a thing as the freedom of exhaustion. Some
people are so worn down by the yoke of oppression that they
give up. A few years ago in the slum areas of Atlanta, a Negro
guitarist used to sing almost daily: "Ben down so long that down
don't bother me." This is the type of negative freedom and
resignation that often engulfs the life of the oppressed.

But this is not the way out. To accept passively an unjust
system is to coöperate with that system; thereby the oppressed
become as evil as the oppressor. Noncoöperation with evil is as
much a moral obligation as is coöperation with good. The oppressed must never allow the conscience of the oppressor to
slumber. Religion reminds every man that he is his brother's
keeper. To accept injustice or segregation passively is to say to
the oppressor that his actions are morally right. It is a way of
allowing his conscience to fall asleep. At this moment the oppressed fails to be his brother's keeper. So acquiescence—while
often the easier way—is not the moral way. It is the way of the
coward. The Negro cannot win the respect of his oppressor by
acquiescing; he merely increases the oppressor's arrogance and
contempt. Acquiescence is interpreted as proof of the Negro's
inferiority. The Negro cannot win the respect of the white people
of the South or the peoples of the world if he is willing to sell
the future of his children for his personal and immediate comfort and safety. as The entire nation does Today.

A second way that oppressed people sometimes deal with
oppression is to resort to physical violence and corroding hatred.
Violence often brings about momentary results. Nations have
frequently won their independence in battle. But in spite of tem-

porary victories, violence never brings permanent peace. It solves no social problem; it merely creates new and more complicated ones.

Violence as a way of achieving racial justice is both impractical and immoral. It is impractical because it is a descending spiral ending in destruction for all. The old law of an eye for an eye leaves everybody blind. It is immoral because it seeks to humiliate the opponent rather than win his understanding; it seeks to annihilate rather than to convert. Violence is immoral because it thrives on hatred rather than love. It destroys community and makes brotherhood impossible. It leaves society in monologue rather than dialogue. Violence ends by defeating itself. It creates bitterness in the survivors and brutality in the destroyers. A voice echoes through time saying to every potential Peter, "Put up your sword." History is cluttered with the wreckage of nations that failed to follow this command.

If the American Negro and other victims of oppression succumb to the temptation of using violence in the struggle for freedom, future generations will be the recipients of a desolate night of bitterness, and our chief legacy to them will be an endless reign of meaningless chaos. Violence is not the way.

The third way open to oppressed people in their quest for freedom is the way of nonviolent resistance. Like the synthesis in Hegelian philosophy, the principle of nonviolent resistance seeks to reconcile the truths of two opposites—acquiescence and violence—while avoiding the extremes and immoralities of both. The nonviolent resister agrees with the person who acquiesces that one should not be physically aggressive toward his opponent but he balances the equation by agreeing with the person of violence that evil must be resisted. He avoids the nonresistance of the former and the violent resistance of the latter. With nonviolent resistance, <u>no individual or group need submit to any</u> <u>wrong, nor need anyone resort to violence in order to right a</u> <u>wrong.</u>

It seems to me that this is the method that must guide the actions of the Negro in the present crisis in race relations. Through nonviolent resistance the Negro will be able to rise to the noble height of opposing the unjust system while loving the perpetrators of the system. The Negro must work passionately and unrelentingly for full stature as a citizen, but he must not use inferior methods to gain it. He must never come to terms with falsehood, malice, hate, or destruction.

Nonviolent resistance makes it possible for the Negro to remain in the South and struggle for his rights. The Negro's problem will not be solved by running away. He cannot listen to the glib suggestion of those who would urge him to migrate en masse to other sections of the country. By grasping his great opportunity in the South he can make a lasting contribution to the moral strength of the nation and set a sublime example of courage for generations yet unborn.

By nonviolent resistance, the Negro can also enlist all men of good will in his struggle for equality. The problem is not a purely racial one, with Negroes set against whites. In the end, it is not a struggle between people at all, but a tension between justice and injustice. Nonviolent resistance is not aimed against oppressors but against oppression. Under its banner consciences, not racial groups, are enlisted.

If the Negro is to achieve the goal of integration, he must organize himself into a militant and nonviolent mass movement. All three elements are indispensable. The movement for equality and justice can only be a success if it has both a mass and militant character; the barriers to be overcome require both. Nonviolence is an imperative in order to bring about ultimate community.

A mass movement of a militant quality that is not at the same time committed to nonviolence tends to generate conflict, which in turn breeds anarchy. The support of the participants and the sympathy of the uncommitted are both inhibited by the threat that bloodshed will engulf the community. This reaction in turn encourages the opposition to threaten and resort to force. When, however, the mass movement repudiates violence while moving resolutely toward its goal, its opponents are revealed as the instigators and practitioners of violence if it occurs. Then public support is magnetically attracted to the advocates of nonviolence, while those who employ violence are literally disarmed by overwhelming sentiment against their stand.

Only through a nonviolent approach can the fears of the white community be mitigated. A guilt-ridden white minority lives in fear that if the Negro should ever attain power, he would act without restraint or pity to revenge the injustices and brutality of the years. It is something like a parent who continually mistreats a son. One day that parent raises his hand to strike the son, only to discover that the son is now as tall as he is. The parent is suddenly afraid—fearful that the son will use his new physical power to repay his parent for all the blows of the past.

The Negro, once a helpless child, has now grown up politically, culturally, and economically. Many white men fear retaliation. The job of the Negro is to show them that they have nothing to fear, that the Negro understands and forgives and is ready to forget the past. He must convince the white man that all he seeks is justice, *for both himself and the white man.* A mass movement exercising nonviolence is an object lesson in power under discipline, a demonstration to the white community that if such a movement attained a degree of strength, it would use its power creatively and not vengefully.

Nonviolence can touch men where the law cannot reach them.

When the law regulates behavior it plays an indirect part in molding public sentiment. The enforcement of the law is itself a form of peaceful persuasion. But the law needs help. The courts can order desegregation of the public schools. But what can be done to mitigate the fears, to disperse the hatred, violence, and irrationality gathered around school integration, to take the initiative out of the hands of racial demagogues, to release respect for the law? In the end, for laws to be obeyed, men must believe they are right.

Here nonviolence comes in as the ultimate form of persuasion. It is the method which seeks to implement the just law by appealing to the conscience of the great decent majority who through blindness, fear, pride, or irrationality have allowed their consciences to sleep.

The nonviolent resisters can summarize their message in the following simple terms: We will take direct action against injustice without waiting for other agencies to act. We will not obey unjust laws or submit to unjust practices. We will do this peacefully, openly, cheerfully because our aim is to persuade. We adopt the means of nonviolence because our end is a community at peace with itself. We will try to persuade with our words, but if our words fail, we will try to persuade with our acts. We will always be willing to talk and seek fair compromise, but we are ready to suffer when necessary and even risk our lives to become witnesses to the truth as we see it.

The way of nonviolence means a willingness to suffer and sacrifice. It may mean going to jail. If such is the case the resister must be willing to fill the jail houses of the South. It may even mean physical death. But if physical death is the price that a man must pay to free his children and his white brethren from a permanent death of the spirit, then nothing could be more redemptive.

What is the Negro's best defense against acts of violence inflicted upon him? As Dr. Kenneth Clark has said so eloquently, "His only defense is to meet every act of barbarity, illegality, cruelty and injustice toward an individual Negro with the fact that 100 more Negroes will present themselves in his place as potential victims." Every time one Negro school teacher is fired for believing in integration, a thousand others should be ready to take the same stand. If the oppressors bomb the home of one Negro for his protest, they must be made to realize that to press back the rising tide of the Negro's courage they will have to bomb hundreds more, and even then they will fail.

Faced with this dynamic unity, this amazing self-respect, this willingness to suffer, and this refusal to hit back, the oppressor will find, as oppressors have always found, that he is glutted with his own barbarity. Forced to stand before the world and his God splattered with the blood of his brother, he will call an end to his self-defeating massacre.

American Negroes must come to the point where they can say to their white brothers, paraphrasing the words of Gandhi: "We will match your capacity to inflict suffering with our capacity to endure suffering. We will meet your physical force with soul force. We will not hate you, but we cannot in all good conscience obey your unjust laws. Do to us what you will and we will still love you. Bomb our homes and threaten our children; send your hooded perpetrators of violence into our communities and drag us out on some wayside road, beating us and leaving us half dead, and we will still love you. But we will soon wear you down by our capacity to suffer. And in winning our freedom we will so appeal to your heart and conscience that we will win you in the process."

Realism impels me to admit that many Negroes will find it difficult to follow the path of nonviolence. Some will consider it senseless; some will argue that they have neither the strength nor the courage to join in such a mass demonstration of nonviolent action. As E. Franklin Frazier points out in *Black Bourgeoisie,* many Negroes are occupied in a middle-class struggle for status and prestige. They are more concerned about "conspicuous consumption" than about the cause of justice, and are probably not prepared for the ordeals and sacrifices involved in nonviolent action. Fortunately, however, the success of this method is not dependent on its unanimous acceptance. A few Negroes in every community, unswervingly committed to the nonviolent way, can persuade hundreds of others at least to use nonviolence as a technique and serve as the moral force to awaken the slumbering national conscience. Thoreau was thinking of such a creative minority when he said: "I know this well, that if one thousand, if one hundred, if ten men whom I could name—if ten honest men only—aye, if one honest man, in the state of Massachusetts, ceasing to hold slaves, were actually to withdraw from the copartnership, and be locked up in the county jail therefore, it would be the abolition of slavery in America. For it matters not how small the beginning may seem to be, what is once well done is done forever."

Mahatma Gandhi never had more than one hundred persons absolutely committed to his philosophy. But with this small group of devoted followers, he galvanized the whole of India, and through a magnificent feat of nonviolence challenged the might of the British Empire and won freedom for his people.

This method of nonviolence will not work miracles overnight. Men are not easily moved from their mental ruts, their prejudiced and irrational feelings. When the underprivileged demand freedom, the privileged first react with bitterness and resistance. Even when the demands are couched in nonviolent terms, the initial response is the same. Nehru once remarked that the British were never so angry as when the Indians resisted them with nonviolence, that he never saw eyes so full of hate as those of the

British troops to whom he turned the other cheek when they beat him with lathis. But nonviolent resistance at least changed the minds and hearts of the Indians, however impervious the British may have appeared. "We cast away our fear," says Nehru. And in the end the British not only granted freedom to India but came to have a new respect for the Indians. Today a mutual friendship based on complete equality exists between these two peoples within the Commonwealth.

In the South too, the initial white reaction to Negro resistance has been bitter. I do not predict that a similar happy ending will come to Montgomery in a few months, because integration is more complicated than independence. But I know that the Negroes of Montgomery are already walking straighter because of the protest. And I expect that this generation of Negro children throughout the United States will grow up stronger and better because of the courage, the dignity, and the suffering of the nine children of Little Rock, and their counterparts in Nashville, Clinton, and Sturges. And I believe that the white people of this country are being affected too, that beneath the surface this nation's conscience is being stirred.

The nonviolent approach does not immediately change the heart of the oppressor. It first does something to the hearts and souls of those committed to it. It gives them new self-respect; it calls up resources of strength and courage that they did not know they had. Finally it reaches the opponent and so stirs his conscience that reconciliation becomes a reality.

I suggest this approach because I think it is the only way to reëstablish the broken community. Court orders and federal enforcement agencies will be of inestimable value in achieving desegregation. But desegregation is only a partial, though necessary, step toward the ultimate goal which we seek to realize. Desegregation will break down the legal barriers, and bring men together physically. But something must happen so to touch the hearts and souls of men that they will come together, not because the law says it, but because it is natural and right. In other words, our ultimate goal is integration which is genuine intergroup and interpersonal living. Only through nonviolence can this goal be attained, for the aftermath of nonviolence is reconciliation and the creation of the beloved community.

It is becoming clear that the Negro is in for a season of suffering. As victories for civil rights mount in the federal courts, angry passions and deep prejudices are further aroused. The mountain of state and local segregation laws still stands. Negro leaders continue to be arrested and harassed under city ordinances, and their homes continue to be bombed. State laws continue to be enacted to circumvent integration. I pray that, recognizing the necessity of suffering, the Negro will make of it a virtue. To suffer in a righteous cause is to grow to our humanity's full stature. If only to save himself from bitterness, the Negro needs the vision to see the ordeals of this generation as the opportunity to transfigure himself and American society. If he has to go to jail for the cause of freedom, let him enter it in the fashion Gandhi urged his countrymen, "as the bridegroom enters the bride's chamber"— that is, with a little trepidation but with a great expectation.

Nonviolence is a way of humility and self-restraint. We Negroes talk a great deal about our rights, and rightly so. We proudly proclaim that three-fourths of the people of the world are colored. We have the privilege of watching in our generation the great drama of freedom and independence as it unfolds in Asia and Africa. All of these things are in line with the work of providence. We must be sure, however, that we accept them in the right spirit. In an effort to achieve freedom in America, Asia, and Africa we must not try to leap from a position of disadvantage to one of advantage, thus subverting justice. We must seek democracy and not the substitution of one tyranny for another. Our aim must never be to defeat or humiliate the white man. We must not become victimized with a philosophy of black supremacy. God is not interested merely in the freedom of black men, and brown men, and yellow men; God is interested in the freedom of the whole human race.

The nonviolent approach provides an answer to the long debated question of gradualism *versus* immediacy. On the one hand it prevents one from falling into the sort of patience which is an excuse for do-nothingism and escapism, ending up in standstillism. On the other hand it saves one from the irresponsible words which estrange without reconciling and the hasty judgment which is blind to the necessities of social process. It recognizes the need for moving toward the goal of justice with wise restraint and calm reasonableness. But it also recognizes the immorality of slowing up in the move toward justice and capitulating to the guardians of an unjust status quo. It recognizes that social change cannot come overnight. But it causes one to work as if it were a possibility the next morning.

Through nonviolence we avoid the temptation of taking on the psychology of victors. Thanks largely to the noble and invaluable work of the NAACP, we have won great victories in the federal courts. But we must not be self-satisfied. We must respond to every decision with an understanding of those who have opposed us, and with acceptance of the new adjustments that the court orders pose for them. We must act in such a way that our victories will be triumphs for good will in all men, white and Negro.

Nonviolence is essentially a positive concept. Its corollary must always be growth. On the one hand nonviolence requires noncooperation with evil; on the other hand it requires coöperation with the constructive forces of good. Without this constructive aspect noncoöperation ends where it begins. Therefore, the Negro must get to work on a program with a broad range of positive goals.

One point in the Negro's program should be a plan to improve his own economic lot. Through the establishment of credit unions, savings and loan associations, and coöperative enterprises the Negro can greatly improve his economic status. He must develop habits of thrift and techniques of wise investment. He must not wait for the end of the segregation that lies at the basis of his economic deprivation; he must act now to lift himself up by his own bootstraps.

The constructive program ahead must include a campaign to get Negroes to register and vote. Certainly they face many external barriers. All types of underhand methods are still being used in the South to prevent the Negroes from voting, and the success of these efforts is not only unjust, it is a real embarrassment to the nation we love and must protect. The advocacy of free elections in Europe by American officials is hypocrisy when free elections are not held in great sections of America.

But external resistance is not the only present barrier to Negro voting. Apathy among the Negroes themselves is also a factor. Even where the polls are open to all, Negroes have shown themselves too slow to exercise their voting privileges. There must be a concerted effort on the part of Negro leaders to arouse their people from their apathetic indifference to this obligation of citizenship. In the past, apathy was a moral failure. Today, it is a form of moral and political suicide.

The constructive program ahead must include a vigorous attempt to improve the Negro's personal standards. It must be reiterated that the standards of the Negro as a group lag behind not because of an inherent inferiority, but because of the fact that segregation does exist. The "behavior deviants" within the Negro community stem from the economic deprivation, emotional frustration, and social isolation which are the inevitable concomitants of segregation. When the white man argues that segregation should continue because of the Negro's lagging standards, he fails to see that the standards lag because of segregation.

Yet Negroes must be honest enough to admit that our standards do often fall short. One of the sure signs of maturity is the ability to rise to the point of self-criticism. Whenever we are objects of criticism from white men, even though the criticisms are maliciously directed and mixed with half-truths, we must pick out the elements of truth and make them the basis of creative reconstruction. We must not let the fact that we are the victims of injustice lull us into abrogating responsibility for our own lives.

Our crime rate is far too high. Our level of cleanliness is frequently far too low. Too often those of us who are in the middle class live above our means, spend money on nonessentials and frivolities, and fail to give to serious causes, organizations, and educational institutions that so desperately need funds. We are too often loud and boisterous, and spend far too much on drink. Even the most poverty-stricken among us can purchase a ten-cent bar of soap; even the most uneducated among us can have high morals. Through community agencies and religious institutions Negro leaders must develop a positive program through which Negro youth can become adjusted to urban living and improve their general level of behavior. Since crime often grows out of a sense of futility and despair, Negro parents must be urged to give their children the love, attention, and sense of belonging that a segregated society deprives them of. By improving our standards here and now we will go a long way toward breaking down the arguments of the segregationist.

This then must be our present program: Nonviolent resistance to all forms of racial injustice, including state and local laws and practices, even when this means going to jail; and imaginative, bold, constructive action to end the demoralization caused by the legacy of slavery and segregation, inferior schools, slums, and second-class citizenship. The nonviolent struggle, if conducted with the dignity and courage already shown by the people of Montgomery and the children of Little Rock, will in itself help end the demoralization; but a new frontal assault on the poverty, disease, and ignorance of a people too long ignored by America's conscience will make victory more certain.

In short, we must work on two fronts. On the one hand, we must continue to resist the system of segregation which is the basic cause of our lagging standards; on the other hand we must work constructively to improve the standards themselves. There must be a rhythmic alternation between attacking the causes and healing the effects.

This is a great hour for the Negro. The challenge is here. To become the instruments of a great idea is a privilege that history gives only occasionally. Arnold Toynbee says in A *Study of History* that it may be the Negro who will give the new spiritual dynamic to Western civilization that it so desperately needs to survive. I hope this is possible. The spiritual power that the Negro can radiate to the world comes from love, understanding, good will, and nonviolence. It may even be possible for the Negro, through adherence to nonviolence, so to challenge the nations of the world that they will seriously seek an alternative to war and destruction. In a day when Sputniks and Explorers dash through outer space and guided ballistic missiles are carving highways of death through the stratosphere, nobody can win a war. Today the choice is no longer between violence and nonviolence. It is either nonviolence or nonexistence. The Negro may be God's appeal to this age—an age drifting rapidly to its doom. The eternal appeal takes the form of a warning: "All who take the sword will perish by the sword."

Appendix

NEGOTIATING COMMITTEE

Rev. Ralph D. Abernathy
Rev. L. Roy Bennett
Mr. Fred D. Gray, Att'y.
Rev. H. H. Hubbard
Dr. Moses W. Jones*
Rev. Martin Luther King, Jr.
Mr. Charles Langford, Att'y.
Mr. Rufus A. Lewis
Mr. E. D. Nixon
Mr. J. E. Pierce
Mrs. Jo Ann Robinson
Rev. S. S. Seay*
Mrs. A. W. West
Rev. A. W. Wilson

EXECUTIVE BOARD

Rev. Ralph D. Abernathy
Mrs. Euretta Adair
Rev. A. W. Alford
Rev. L. Roy Bennett
Rev. R. B. Binion
Mr. P. M. Blair
Rev. J. W. Bonner
Miss Ida Caldwell
Dr. James Caple*
Rev. J. H. Cherry*
Rev. H. A. L. Clement*
Mr. P. E. Conley
Mrs. Erna A. Dungee
Mr. Isaiah Ferguson*
Rev. U. J. Fields
Rev. E. N. French
Rev. R. J. Glasco
Rev. Robert Graetz*

Mr. Fred D. Gray, Att'y.
Mr. Thomas Gray
Rev. J. W. Hayes
Rev. R. W. Hilson
Rev. H. H. Hubbard
Rev. H. H. Johnson
Dr. Moses W. Jones
Rev. Martin Luther King, Jr.
Rev. B. D. Lambert
Mrs. Charles Langford, Att'y.
Mr. Clarence W. Lee
Mr. Rufus A. Lewis
Mr. E. H. Ligon*
Mrs. Jimmie Lowe*
Mr. R. L. Matthews
Rev. A. W. Murphy*
Rev. H. J. Palmer
Mrs. Rosa Parks
Mr. J. E. Pierce
Rev. W. J. Powell
Mrs. Jo Ann Robinson
Rev. A. Sanders
Rev. S. S. Seay
Rev. B. J. Simms*
Dr. Jefferson Underwood*
Mrs. A. W. West
Rev. A. W. Wilson

OFFICERS OF THE MIA
Original

Rev. Martin Luther King, Jr.,
President
Rev. L. Roy Bennett, Vice-
President

* Added after original formation.

Rev. E. N. French, Corresponding
Secretary
Rev. U. J. Fields, Recording
Secretary
Mrs. Erna A. Dungee, Financial
Secretary
Mr. E. D. Nixon, Treasurer

Current

Rev. Martin Luther King, Jr.,
President
Rev. W. J. Powell, 1st Vice-
President
Dr. Moses W. Jones, 2nd Vice-
President
Rev. Robert Graetz, Secretary
Mrs. Erna A. Dungee, Financial
Secretary
Rev. A. W. Wilson, Treasurer
Mr. J. E. Pierce, Parliamentarian
Rev. Ralph D. Abernathy, Chair-
man of Executive Board
Rev. S. S. Seay, Executive
Secretary

FINANCE COMMITTEE
Original

Mrs. Euretta Adair
Rev. R. B. Binion
Mr. P. M. Blair
Miss Ida Caldwell
Mrs. Erna A. Dungee
Rev. R. J. Glasco

Rev. J. W. Hayes
Rev. H. H. Johnson
Mr. E. D. Nixon
Rev. W. J. Powell

Current

Rev. H. H. Hubbard, Chairman
Rev. R. B. Binion
Mr. P. M. Blair
Mrs. Erna A. Dungee
Rev. H. H. Johnson
Mr. Clarence W. Lee
Rev. A. W. Wilson

TRANSPORTATION
COMMITTEE

Mr. Rufus A. Lewis, Chairman
Mrs. Euretta Adair
Mr. P. E. Conley
Rev. R. J. Glasco
Rev. J. W. Hayes
Rev. H. J. Palmer
Rev. W. J. Powell
Rev. A. Sanders
Rev. B. J. Simms*

PROGRAM COMMITTEE

Rev. Ralph D. Abernathy,
Chairman
Rev. L. Roy Bennett
Rev. H. H. Hubbard
Mrs. Rosa Parks
Mrs. A. W. West

* Added after original formation.

Index

Lewis, Rufus A., 30, 34, 56, 72-73,
77, 79
Lincoln, Abraham, 193
Little Rock, Arkansas, 10
Central High School, 10
Livingston, Sonny Kyle, 179-180
Lloyds of London, 158
Locke, John, 92
Lucy, Autherine, 156
Lynn, Judge, of Birmingham, 152

Marshall, Thurgood, 145
Marx, Karl, 92, 94-95, 97
Maryland State Baptist Center, 38
Matthews, R. L., 34
Mays, Benjamin E., 145-146
Men of Montgomery, The, 121-122,
169-170, 177
Methodist Church of Montgomery,
116
Mill, John Stuart, 92, 97
Minneapolis Tribune, The, 124
Montgomery Advertiser, The, 49,
85, 124, 174, 176, 184
Montgomery Baptist Association, 83
Montgomery Chamber of Commerce,
27
Montgomery City Jail, 128
Montgomery City Lines, 41, 113,
118, 182
Montgomery County Court, 179
Montgomery County Grand Jury,
142, 179
Montgomery Improvement Associa-
tion (MIA), 57, 73-74, 77, 80-
83, 89, 108, 113-114, 116-118,
122, 125, 142, 153-155, 157,
159, 163, 169, 171, 180, 188
MIA Newsletter, 78
Montgomery Protesters, 192
Moral Man and Immoral Society, 98
Morehouse College, 91, 141, 145
Morgan, Miss Juliette, 85
Mt. Olive Baptist Church of Mont-
gomery, 176
Muelder, Dean Walter, 100

Muste, Dr. A. J., 95
Myrdal, Gunnar, 205

National Association for the Ad-
vancement of Colored People
(NAACP), 29-34, 39, 43-44, 56,
81, 145, 152, 186, 192-193, 221
National City Lines, Inc., 113-114,
119
National Council of Churches, 208
Negro Citizens Committee, 57
Negro History Bulletin, The, 11
Negro Trinity Lutheran Church of
Montgomery, 74
New England Conservatory, 23
Niebuhr, Reinhold, 97-100
Nietzsche, F. W., 96-97
Nixon, E. D., 34, 38-39, 44-46, 55-
57, 72, 140, 160, 173

Old Ship A.M.E. Zion Church of
Montgomery, 48

Parker, Rev. Henry, 115, 118, 120-
121
Parks, Commissioner Frank A., 109,
111-112
Parks, Mrs. Rosa, 43-47, 55, 61, 63,
69, 110
Patterson, Rev. Merle, 177
Perkins, Mrs. Della, 148
Phenomenology of Mind, 100
Philosophy of History, 100
Philosophy of Right, 100
Pierce, J. E., 73
Plato, 92
Plessy Doctrine, 152
Pope, Dean Liston, 207
Powell, Rev. W. J., 48, 73
Progressive Democrats, 34

Rauschenbusch, Walter, 91-92
Reddick, L. D., 181
Reeves, Jeremiah, 31-32
Robertson, Allen, 178
Robinson, Mrs. Jo Ann, 30, 34, 73,
118